What People are Saying About
No Matter Which Way You Turn

Both Tina (Ms. T) and I thoroughly enjoyed "Tales from the Deer Blind". The humor and insightful "look under the hood" of a Conservation Officer's more memorable efforts was very entertaining. It seems it's not just the violators of game laws that can spin a yarn. And fortunately Wayne's new effort "No Matter Which Way You Turn" looks to be more of the same.

—Kyle and Tina Randall
Wilderness Journal Television

The trials and tribulations of being a Michigan Conservation Officer are presented very colorfully and accurately in No Matter Which Way You Turn. Officer Coleman's attention to detail and recollection of how events really happened brought me back to my days as a CO in the field. Wayne captures the very essence of the Game Warden through his vast knowledge and witty sense of humor.

—Scott Berg,
Michigan Conservation Officer, Retired

Now that I've finished reading retired conservation Officer Wayne Coleman's first book, Tales from the Deer Blind, I can't wait to read his second, No Matter Which Way You Turn. The last chapters of Tales from the Deer Blind were some of the most spell binding in the book because they dealt with life-threatening situations he faced. A carefully placed teaser at the end of the book that is part of a chapter titled Close Calls in No Matter Which Way You Turn, has me wondering how the story he started ends!

—Richard P. Smith
Outdoor Writer/Photographer
Marquette, Michigan

No Matter Which Way You Turn

A Game Warden's Memoir
Part Two

WAYNE COLEMAN

Book design by Maureen Cutajar
www.gopublished.com

ISBN 13: 978-1514207161
ISBN 10: 1514207168

Acknowledgements

No Matter Which Way You Turn would never have come to be without the encouragement and insistence of prize-winning writer William E. Peterson. Author of two books that relate his experiences as a crew chief in Vietnam, Bill served as a Volunteer Conservation Officer during my tenure in Menominee County. This author, war veteran, builder, business man, pilot, and all around Good Man in the Woods was much more than a friend; serving by my side as a partner and backup officer, more than once helping me out of a dangerous situation. His help in writing, editing and publishing this, my second book, has been priceless. Thank you, Bill.

Thanks to the many good citizens of Menominee County who, having read my first book, Tales from the Deer Blind, contacted me with numerous new story ideas for *No Matter Which Way You Turn*. Some were those who became friends after being arrested by me, wanting the story of their capture to be chronicled in the new book.

My dear wife Katherine has been by my side since 1970 and

has been my mainstay through it all. She has served as *Mrs. Game Warden,* dealing with the public, answering the phone, raising the Game Warden's kids putting up with a degree of abuse from the public, and enduring my rabid excitement about my career. Through it all she constantly encouraged me to write of my experiences. *No Matter Which Way You Turn* is the second result of her support.

Special thanks are due to fellow conservation officers who instructed, shared their experiences, and served by my side. Thanks to all the *old school* Game Wardens. The world will never see the likes of you again.

Thanks to the officers from other agencies: The Michigan State Police, Sheriff's deputies, city and village officers were invaluable backup and assistance along the way. Thanks to those who rode with me and allowed me the honor of patrolling along with them.

Thanks to the citizens of the State of Michigan whose support and wise use of our natural resources provided me the best career I could ever have dreamed of living.

Thank you, good and faithful reader. May you enjoy each and every story.

Contents

Foreword

Growing up in the village of Carney in Michigan's Upper Peninsula, it was natural for me to develop a love for the outdoors and all the good things offered by its many natural resources. Menominee County was a paradise for hunters and fishermen, and the local Conservation Officer was an integral part of our community.

The Game Warden was a member of the Lions Club, the volunteer fire department, and he attended the local church with his family. His children attended school and played sports with ours. It was only normal to expect that when Wayne Coleman was assigned to Menominee County, I would soon make his acquaintance.

After meeting while fishing on the Big Cedar River I applied and was accepted as a Volunteer Conservation Officer, assigned to work with Wayne.

Many interesting and happy hours were spent riding "shotgun" in Officer Coleman's patrol car, tracking natural resource law offenders through the forest, or chasing Salmon snaggers along the stream bank.

Through this experience I learned that the career of the Conservation Officer is interesting, active, varied, and not always easy or fun. As a Vietnam veteran I enjoyed the spirit of the chase once more while working with Wayne Coleman those years during the 1980's

Such dedication to the enforcement of our natural resource laws is not often found, and Officer Coleman's skills in interacting with the public made having one's license checked a pleasure.

His book brings back many memories of those times, and it's a true joy to relive the old experiences through the stories.

Author's Note

The following stories are based on true happenings. Many of the names have been changed to save the good citizens of the State of Michigan the embarrassment of admitting having known me. If at some point these narrations can serve to entertain, inspire, inform or motivate the reader, I shall consider my life's work accomplished.

A Family Affair

The private life of a Conservation officer's family differs slightly from that of police officers of other agencies in that it's, well, really not all that private. The average police officer comes home from working his scheduled shift, sheds his uniform and enjoys relative freedom from his career until it's time to once again go to work. For the game warden his free time is often interrupted by citizens calling with questions concerning recreation laws or complaints that must be answered. On occasion someone may simply show up unannounced at the residence wanting to conduct some type of natural resource business. These aspects of the job are usually accepted by the warden and his/her family as part of the life they were assigned when the hand was raised and the oath of office spoken.

The position of the CO is unique in that, in contrast with other agencies, there is only one officer assigned to enforce the natural resource laws for areas as large as several counties. A citizen observing a blue or black-and-white patrol car as a rule does not know which police officer is in the neighborhood. If the pickup truck of a conservation officer passes by most people know the identity of the driver because he's the only one for miles around. They also know that his phone number is in the book and that they may contact him at any time, day or night. If the CO is not at home, his wife or one of the kids will advise how the officer may be reached. In recent years the State policy has relaxed somewhat and CO's have been given some relief. Phone numbers can be unlisted and complaints are handled through the Report All Poaching hotline, referring violations to officers who are on duty rather than calling a CO from his off duty time.

One of the few things that I have done right in my years of stumbling around this planet was to teach my children the sport of distance running. Running teaches patience, stamina, courage and the deserved feeling of a job well done. Daughter Rebecca took to running like a retriever to water, relishing in the sweat, the fatigue, the victory over set goals. Luckily this prepared her for the abuse she occasionally encountered because of her father's occupation. Though she will deny it, she is the spitfire of the family.

The story was second hand, but I believe the basic tale to be true. One of the 'tough girls' around Stephenson junior high attempted to intimidate Becky over some violation for which I had arrested one of her relatives. After several shoves, trying to goad Becky into a fight, Becky stared her down, saying "In about two seconds there is going to be blood on the pavement, and it won't be mine!" ending the incident.

A natural outdoors person, Becky once astounded her second grade teacher who was holding an exercise concerning the care of tame animals. Questions like "What can you do with a kitten?" and "What can you do with a doggie?" were being answered by the students with "You can pet them, you can feed them, and you can give them a bath." Wanting to instruct the second graders in the proper care of feeding wild critters such as birds and chipmunks, the teacher asked, "Now class, what can you do with a squirrel?" Becky's hand was the first up. "You shoot them, skin them, cook them, and EAT them!" That garnered a note home and a visit by the game warden to the class taking the pet Ferret and teaching the feeding of small woodland creatures. Becky became a competent archer, bagging two nice deer at age twelve and thirteen; once outshooting and embarrassing her husband and father-in-law in their attempt at instructing the supposed incompetent Becky in the art of archery.

Today Becky home schools her two children and is an avid runner, entering races from the 5K to marathons. Both of the grand kids are runners, and are instructed in the Christian life as they conduct their studies at home.

Son Shawn is of a more mild temperament. Once when he was the target of physical bullying I visited the office of the superintendent of the high school. I advised them that three boys were hiding behind the bleachers when students walked the hundred yards from one school to another. They would grab Shawn, push him down and proceed to punch and kick him until the bell rang, sometimes making him late for class. The answer from the superintendent was that if Shawn would only be friendlier, maybe they would stop picking on him. Infuriated, I advised him that I would be waiting in view of the bleachers the next day and defend my child; maybe show the bullies what bullying was really all about. I was told not to worry, that they would take care of the problem, and they did.

On another occasion I was approached by Shawn while I was working on the patrol boat.

"Dad, have you even been in a fight?" asked Shawn.

"Not very often," I answered, not wanting to reveal to my young son that sometimes physical contact with law breakers was necessary. "Why do you ask?"

"Well, I was just wondering what you would do," he said.

"If it's necessary you have to make it fast. You have to let the bad guy know that you're the boss. Take his feet out from under him if you can. Get the cuffs on him and put him in the patrol car. The faster you get him to jail the better. Does that answer your question?"

"Sure, thanks dad," answered Shawn.

The next day I was in the shop sharpening the chainsaw. Shawn came in, eager to share some news.

"Dad, your advice worked," he began.

"What are you talking about?" I asked.

"Well, Clint has been picking on me; punching me and pushing me around, no matter what I tried to make him stop. Today me punched me and pushed me down."

"So what did you do?" I asked, afraid of what I might hear.

"I got up and told him, 'My dad says to make this fast.'" he said. "Then I tripped him and knocked him down. I kicked him a couple of times as hard as I could. By then he was up and running too fast for me to catch him."

"Now son, I don't want you to...."

"No dad, it was great," Shawn interrupted. "He ran away from me like a cat from a vacuum cleaner. Then just before we got on the bus he came up to me and said he wanted for us to be friends."

"Well, okay," I said. "But don't start thinking that this is the only way to resolve conflict."

"Okay dad."

"Do you have any other questions?" I asked.

"Yeah. How do they make peanut butter?"

While I will admit that I was not present nearly enough during the formative years of my children, I did attempt to teach them right from wrong, and would occasionally take Shawn along on patrol during his high school years. Sometimes when we were together while I was off duty we would encounter some violation that could not be ignored and he would be present during some pretty good adventures as I made the arrest. I had no idea that he would be picking up on what we often referred to as "The tricks of the trade."

Both Shawn and Becky ran track and cross-country. Cross-country was more a family than a team, each member supporting the others more closely than in many other sports. When Shawn was a senior, word got around that he was involved in TP'ing peoples' houses. At first I was angry, but the explanation was that if a cross-country team member skipped practice, the rest of the team would sneak up on the absentee's house and TP the trees in the yard in retribution for the misdeed of the 'slacker'. That changed my thinking. If that was the worst thing my son was involved in, I was pretty lucky.

One fall afternoon at cross-country practice I overheard a runner grousing about the team getting caught by the father of a runner who made the boys come back and clean up all the toilet paper from his yard. I said that Shawn hadn't mentioned anything about getting caught, and the runner said "Of course he didn't get caught. He drives without lights!" Now where did he learn that? It was also related to me that Shawn once drove without lights to evade a bully who had intended to do him serious bodily harm. That bully was later arrested for other violations, but that's another story.

It was my dear wife who had the most difficult job of all. While I was out playing grownup Cops and Robbers she raised two children, ran the household, took care of the finances, answered the phone and attempted to answer many difficult questions about the law. She was "Mrs. Game Warden", on duty twenty-four hours a day and subject to much of the same abuse that I myself encountered on the job.

Many a supper grew cold as my duties kept me late. Many a Thanksgiving and Christmas dinner were interrupted as I was called away to arrest another form of "turkey" who had chosen the holiday to break the law, thinking he would be free of police interference. Through it all Kathy bore the aspects of a CO's life with patience.

In public she had to endure the same old game warden jokes on and on, ad infinitum. On the rare occasions in which I might have had a close call she would hear the wives of other officers speak as if she was not even in the room: "My husband would have just shot them." "My husband wouldn't have messed around with those violators." "My husband wouldn't have screwed up like that." Through it all she endured it with unbelievable grace. By the time the kids were in high school she applied and was hired as a State Park ranger, serving for fourteen years with the DNR.

Today I am told that the average CO lives a personal life that is more remote from the public. Phone numbers can be unlisted, work goes according to scheduled hours, and the family is less under the public microscope. While I laud this new lifestyle for the officers, if I were back on the force I would miss that call in the night, jarring me awake and taking me on some new, yet to be experienced adventure.

Uninvited Guests

When it comes to controversial animals, the skunk ranks right up close to number one. While many members of the animal kingdom are easily placed in varying levels of desirability, skunks occupy both ends of the 'good' versus 'bad' spectrum. Honey bees are referred to as the Angels of Agriculture. Wolverines are described in terms of evil incarnate. Everybody else takes their place somewhere in between. Mention the skunk however, and the reaction will be either very positive, or very negative.

On side one you have a loveable creature; cute, cuddly and friendly. Cartoons portray them as having one stripe down the back with a luxurious, full, squirrel like tail. While other animal friends acknowledge their little friend's propensity for being somewhat odoriferous, that aspect is usually overlooked in good humor and Mr. Skunk is welcomed as a member of the cartoon animal community. Skunks are often kept as pets and are easily domesticated. Even wild skunks can sometimes be seen eating cat food from an outside feeding dish right along with the family cat.

Skunks are veritable insect pest control machines. While they may tear your lawn up, they will rid your turf of grubs. They are very effective in ridding your property of ground hornets and wasps. How they can capture and eat hornets at night from their nests without getting stung has always been a mystery to me. They must know which end to bite first. Mice, grasshoppers and snakes make up a large part of their diet. Being omnivorous they will eat almost anything including vegetables, carrion and under certain conditions, their own kind.

Contrary to popular belief, skunks do not readily spray anyone and everyone in their path. Barking, attacking dogs are likely to become victims, and understandably so. Humans can avoid being sprayed by simply making a quiet retreat if possible. Having poor eyesight, the skunk may not even see a person, but will usually give some warning by hissing or foot stamping before resorting to more serious measures.

On side two, skunks do indeed rip up a lot of lawn in their quest for grubs, and their love for insects often extends to honey bees. A hungry skunk can rid a bee keeper's hive completely of bees in just a few nights. Scratching at the hive entrance, the skunk will catch and eat the bees as they sally forth to defend their home. As members of the weasel family skunks also love eggs, and are not opposed to raiding the farmer's chicken house. The theory concerning their spreading rabies is a coin toss. In my entire career in Menominee County I did not encounter a single case of rabies. This not to say that there were no incidents of skunk borne rabies, but if so, they were certainly rare.

The biggest problem with skunks is their uncanny ability to move in and set up housekeeping where they are not welcome. Skunks seem to love the shelter of manmade buildings with any sort of access between the earth and the ground floor. Storage sheds and granaries are usually the buildings of choice because of their seclusion and access to rodents and insects. For some reason, any time a skunk den was discovered in an undesired location, the letters DNR would spring up in bright neon letters in the mind of the victim. The Conservation Officer would be called and the skunks would be live trapped and moved to a more acceptable location.

To trap a skunk, a covered box trap was most often the tool of choice. The animals would readily enter the trap to get a sardine or some peanut butter, and within several days the entire family would be reunited in some remote corner of the state forest. On one occasion the whole family of mamma and five babies were caught in the same trap. This was not known until the moment of release, when the adult paraded out of trap, followed by the troupe of little ones.

Under normal circumstances a new Conservation Officer would learn about skunk control gradually, working with a neighboring officer on complaints. In my case this was not in the cards. I was to learn about these animals the hard way; by having to contend with a family of eight adult sized skunks in our basement during the first winter in our Upper Peninsula home!

Our first house on Wery road had what is known as a Michigan basement. Without any real foundation, the house was built over a hole in the clay and limestone ground. This pit beneath the house served as a well house, furnace room and canned goods pantry. The basement did not reach the outside walls of the building, leaving some eight feet on either side of the house with the floor joists extending to the outside walls, mere inches above the soil. This made an ideal housing location for the skunks in question. I cannot understand why they weren't mentioned in the real estate listing under the heading of 'Many extras'.

Skunks are not true hibernators. They do something called 'winter sleep'. Their metabolism slows somewhat and they are able to snooze for long periods of time without eating. During a January thaw a skunk might be observed foraging about, looking for a snack. With the cooling of the weather the skunk will return to its nest and sleep away the rest of the winter. The skunks under our house spent the first half of the winter undetected. At about eight PM on New Year's Eve the house was suddenly overwhelmed with the horrendous odor of skunk! Our little hidden pals were awake and ready to rumble. Winter conditions kept them all inside, confined to the Michigan basement and shallow space under the floor. There was no time to learn about the humane live trapping and removal of the critters. The battle was on, and they had fired the first volley!

Something must be said about the odor of skunk. A person's usual experience with the smell of skunk is that slight musky odor of garlic that comes wafting through the air vents when the family sedan cruises through an area where a skunk has released its scent. Comments of "Oh, jeez, this is awful," or words to that effect are completely unwarranted, for this is not the true odor of skunk. It's just a teaser; a harbinger of things to come should one choose to get up close and personal with the animal itself. A true dose of skunk spray stings the nostrils and makes the eyes water profusely. Nausea is instantaneous and supper does not want to stay down. After a while the smell seems to disappear but the nausea remains. This means that you've become acclimated to the smell, and it's now just a dull odor that continues to permeate your clothing and everything about you.

A quick trip to the basement, and I do mean 'quick', revealed a skunk standing defiantly in the middle of the basement floor. Retrieving the 22 rifle I dispatched the animal and returned upstairs, confident that I had solved the problem. The increased smell from the dying skunk was hardly noticed, given the ravaged condition of our olfactory faculties.

The skunk could wait until tomorrow to be removed from the basement.

Descending the basement steps the next morning I was horrified to find a second skunk feeding upon the dead carcass of last night's animal control project. Hurrying upstairs I grabbed the sawed-off twelve gauge shotgun and what I thought was a skeet load of number seven shot. The light powder charge in the skeet shot shell would cause minimum damage to the basement walls, or any canned goods that might be encountered by a ricocheting projectile. I don't know why Remington thought it necessary to pack both low powder number seven BB's and magnum number four buckshot both in green shells. Drawing a dead bead on the live skunk and squeezing the trigger I was immediately notified by the sawed off gun that I had chosen the wrong ammunition. With a thunderous blast both skunks were lifted off the basement floor and their pieces plastered against the far wall. Yeah, they stunk. They really stunk badly. By now I can't smell, I can't see, I can't hear, and boy, am I ever gonna catch it when I go upstairs. Not to mention having to clean up the whole smelly mess.

During the next two weeks a total of eight skunks were dispatched by shooting in one form or another. Advice from friends came in profuse abundance. Over the phone, of course. No one came near our home, and we were unable to go anywhere due to the force field put out by our skunk soaked clothing. The phone hardly stopped ringing by well intentioned 'experts'. "Shoot 'em in the spine." "Shoot 'em in the head." "Shoot 'em when their hind feet are off the ground." Believe me, I have tried every conceivable method of shooting skunks, and none of them work. They all smell as soon as they meet their maker.

My supervisor was very understanding, allowing me to do paperwork at home until the problem was resolved. He knew that no neighboring officer would be willing to work with me anyway, and I couldn't blame them.

Eventually all the skunks were gone and we were able to begin the process of cleanup and restoration. All the clothing in the house was washed and washed again. Walls, ceilings and floor were scrubbed. Fumigant was sprayed in every room and the house was closed up for a day, then aired out with the abundant use of open windows and fans. Still the odor persisted. Although we could not smell it, others would immediately mention it should we enter a supermarket or other public building. Often while in uniform it was assumed that I had been called to remove the skunk from whatever restaurant or store I entered. I never told them the difference. Within a month or so things slowly returned to normal.

Skunks occasionally play a humorous role in our everyday lives. Many years ago when I was in grade school one of my friends had a pet skunk. The animal was very tame and enjoyed making the rounds of the community, although the family did not want their pet to cross the highway. One evening a neighbor across the road from the family called to say that the pet skunk was in their yard. My friend's mother walked across the road, picked up the skunk and took it back to their house. Opening their front door she was met by their own skunk standing in the living room! Our neighbor very slow and carefully returned the wild skunk to a far corner of the yard, with profuse apologies.

One of the troopers at the Stephenson state police post was a taxidermist. He had a full body mount of a very lifelike skunk, and I sometimes borrowed it for fun. I might place it in the front seat of the patrol car during the fourth of July parade to surprise people who walked up to the car to talk. I had a lot of fun with that stuffed skunk.

One summer evening a live skunk found its way under our back deck where it was discovered by our dog. She, of course found it necessary to bark until the skunk did what most frightened skunks do. Taking the 22 rifle I put the skunk out of our misery and removed it from under the deck, hoping that the smell would soon leave the house. The next afternoon I was picked up for patrol by my neighboring officer to the south. Upon entering Don's patrol car I apologized for smelling like skunk, even though I could no longer smell it myself.

"I can't smell anything," said Don.

"Well, maybe the smell is all gone then," I said. "Say, can you do me a favor? Just go up to the house and open the door. See if you can smell any skunk odor."

"Sure thing," said Don, whistling as he strolled up to the front door. I had totally forgotten that I had placed the stuffed skunk on the front porch, soon to be taken back to my trooper friend.

Suddenly there was a scream and I looked to see Don slowly walking back to the car, holding his chest with both hands. "There's this big hot spot where my heart used to be!" exclaimed Don. "I opened the door and could smell a faint skunk smell. Then I looked down, and there was that fake skunk right at my feet. You really gotta quit playing with that infernal critter!"

Years have passed, and memories have dimmed somewhat, but the ones involving skunks remain some of the most vivid. Most experiences were interesting and educational. Someday I would once again like to have a stuffed skunk, just for fun. As long as the real ones stay out of my basement!

Close Calls

The maroon 4X4 pickup I had been following had slowed to a crawl. On the narrow two track forest road, by keeping the curves between the truck and the patrol car, it was fairly easy to watch their progress without being detected. The reflection off the side and back windows indicated when they were moving as the warm autumn sun bathed the golden aspens. A slight breeze wafted through the open windows of the patrol car, rattling the dry leaves that were soon to drop from this young poplar stand. Much too nice a day to spend doing paperwork; lots more fun to be out chasing Sunday afternoon road hunters.

The pickup had stopped, signaling their interest in something other than just driving. Hitting the gas I sped up, around the curve and up close behind the stationary truck. The pickup was fairly new with custom high metallic paint and Wisconsin license plates. Both driver and passenger appeared to be in their mid-twenties; the usual profile for many game violators. The passenger's arm was out the window, pointing a handgun at something unseen in the forest. The pistol bucked in his hand as two shots rang out.

Bumping the siren to signal the driver to halt I jumped from the patrol car and ran to the driver's open window, giving my usual "Hold it right there!" greeting for miscreants. The passenger was in the process of desperately trying to unload the hand gun and I shouted for him to put the weapon down. Directing the driver to put the truck in 'park' and hand over the keys I ran to the rear of the vehicle and around to the passenger's side, ordering the passenger to relinquish the hand gun.

The passenger stepped from the truck and stood, pistol in hand. His body language indicated that he did not plan to give up the gun any time soon. Hearing the rustle of dry leaves at the back bumper I turned to see the driver approaching me from behind. Gripping my revolver I started the slow slide of the weapon from its holster.

"Get back around and into the truck!" I shouted to the driver. Then turning back to the passenger, "You! Lay the gun on the ground!"

The passenger did not move, pistol still in hand. The driver continued his slow approach, hands at his side, his fingers twitching like the tail of a feral cat. At the base of my shoulders an icy chill began to creep up the back of my neck, signaling that something very bad was about to happen.

Something had to happen, and fast. At any second the passenger was going to raise his pistol and fire, or the driver was going to attack me from behind, more than likely both at the same time. My heart was hammering and a cold sweat began to trickle down my back inside my shirt. The air was deathly still and the sun seemed to be beating down with a relentless heat. The intensity of the situation would soon be more than any of us could stand.

Jumping to the side I clambered up the low bank that formed the right shoulder of the trail and spun around to face both men. My hand returned to the firm grip on my revolver.

"Drop your gun and get your hands up!" I commanded. "Don't make me use my weapon!"

A sudden look of surprised recognition came to the eyes of the passenger as he suddenly realized the situation he was in, and he dropped the pistol as if it were red hot. Upon my direction both driver and passenger slowly walked around to the front of the patrol car and placed their identifications on the car hood.

"Look man," the driver began, "we didn't mean any harm. You just caught us by surprise."

"Yeah, I wasn't gonna shoot you or anything like that. No way; I'm really sorry. I don't know why I didn't just set the gun down."

"I'd say you panicked, both of you", I said. "We're lucky that things calmed down just in time. We could have had a very unfortunate incident here."

"What are you gonna do with us?" asked the driver.

"Well, I'm sure that you weren't out here to kill yourselves a Game Warden," I said. "Your nonresident small game licenses make it legal for you to hunt. Unfortunately you were hunting from a motor vehicle which as you know, is not legal.

"Now here is the big problem. Wisconsin does not have a registration requirement for hand guns, but Michigan requires that all hand guns brought into the state be registered, so there is no legal way that you can have that pistol here in Michigan. It's a concealed weapons violation and carries heavy penalties such as big fines and jail time. I'm reasonably certain that you were unaware of this, so I'm only going to cite you both for hunting from a motor vehicle.

"You can plead 'guilty' and pay a fine, or you can plead 'not guilty' and we would go to trial. If we go to trial I would have to describe the firearm during testimony and it would come out that you possessed an unregistered hand gun. The last thing I want to do is tell you how to plead, but I really feel that I had to inform you about the concealed weapons law."

"Don't worry about that sir", said the driver. "We're guilty as sin. We really appreciate the break. You won't see us doing this ever again."

"Did you hit whatever it was that you shot at?" I asked.

"No, it was a partridge. Missed him clean."

No report was ever written about this incident. The young Wisconsin hunters went on their way, paying their fines as soon as court opened the next day, and I continued home to get out of that sweat soaked uniform.

Very few police officers ever draw or have to use their sidearm in self-defense during their careers, but every officer survives at least a few 'close calls' which could have developed into tragic incidents if not for luck, training, or the officer's ability to handle critical situations. An officer may be mistaken for game by a hunter. Officers are often called upon to calm a weapon wielding family member in a domestic dispute, or it could be a 'shoot - don't shoot' decision while suddenly facing an armed criminal in any number of scenarios. It's the nature of the occupation, and if we're lucky most of us survive to retire.

One such close call occurred one misty, overcast October morning during the investigation of an illegal, permanent tree stand which had been placed on state land north of the Cherry ridge road in Cedarville Township. The stand was easily located and from a distance it was obvious that it was occupied by a bow hunter. As I approached through the aspen and oak thickets I could see the hunter slowly climbing down from the tree blind. Good. He saw me walking in, and he's coming down to talk. As I approached within forty feet the hunter took his bow and arrow from the drop cord used to lower it from the tree. He then turned around to face me, drawing the bow back in the process.

"Put that bow down!" I shouted reaching for my sidearm.

The hunter immediately let off on the bowstring and removed the arrow. It was a twelve year old boy. The boy was large for his age and easily taken for an adult at a distance. The youngster had climbed down from the tree coincidental to my approach, totally unaware of my presence. Hearing the rustling behind him as I walked up he mistook the sound as that of an approaching deer, and drew back, turning to shoot. I nearly cried with relief. If he had held the bow on me for another second I might have shot him, mistaking him for an assailant. The boy's father was located a short distance away and cited for hunting from an equally illegal permanent tree blind.

Another October day found me enjoying the sunny autumn afternoon forest west of the village of Daggett. A complainant had called stating that one of our annual big buck shooters had been taking deer by shooting them in the neck with a twenty-two rifle to knock them to the ground and killing them with a bow once the deer was down. Momentarily I would be able to observe the secluded field where these violations were allegedly taking place. As silently as possible I approached a vantage point in the oaks on the south side of the opening.

Using a large oak tree for cover I came to the edge of the field. Something about the tree caught my attention, and further observation indicated climbing steps screwed into the side of the tree. Looking up I found myself staring at the pointy end of a hunting arrow nocked into a compound bow held at full draw by a very serious hunter. Hearing my approach he had mistaken my rustling footsteps for those of a deer and waited at full draw for me to appear.

"Oh, now you don't really want to do that now do you?" I asked, trying my best to sound casual.

"Jeepers-crumps! I almost shot you!" It was my complainant, who hadn't expected me to answer the complaint so soon.

"Not to worry. I figured you'd have to check for horns first," I said.

A far more serious incident began one late, cold February night when my pleasant sleep was interrupted by that danged old phone.

"Wayne," said the caller. "There are foot prints in the fresh snow into my cottage out at the river and it looks all smoky inside."

"Why didn't you call the state police or the sheriff?" I asked.

"None of them have a car on the road and I knew you'd come," he answered.

The tracks into the cabin were indeed fresh and the lock on the back door had been jimmied. Upon entering the porch I was greeted by copious clouds of wood smoke. In the middle of the living room floor lay a sleeping form covered by a jacket. Several feet away stood a wastebasket, containing a smoldering fire.

In a fit of rage the cabin owner kicked the sleeping, stocky blonde haired young man who shrieked and rolled over. A glint of chrome caught my eye and I saw a hand reach for what appeared to be a pistol. Two hundred and twenty pounds of Game Warden landing on our pudgy little guest changed his mind about the gun and he was hand cuffed without incident. The occupant of the cabin had apparently called the owner several weeks before and discussed the possibility of his renting the cottage. The owner had agreed to discuss it at a later date, which our subject took as a 'yes' and decided to set up residence without prior approval. Several active warrants for his arrest indicated that he was no stranger to the receiving end of the criminal justice system. He was lodged in the county jail under charges of breaking and entering as well as illegally carrying a concealed weapon. The pistol was identified as a .380 auto, upon which he had been sleeping. There is no doubt in my mind that he would have used it, had he been able to reach it.

The booking, police report and filing of charges occupied most of the day. At 4:00 PM I was driving sleepily north on Highway M-35 on my way home to a shower, shave and a nice long nap. Pulling up and stopping behind the red lights of a Menominee school bus I was surprised to see the car ahead of me pull around and pass the stopped school bus, very nearly missing two children crossing in front of the bus. The pair of students stopped short and jumped back as the car sped past, just missing them by inches. Pulling up abreast of the bus driver I waited for her nod that all was clear before activating my overhead light and siren.

The pursuit lasted for two miles before I overtook the sedan. The driver attempted to convince me that in Wisconsin drivers were not required to stop for school busses taking on or unloading passengers. At that moment the school bus drove past with all students aboard cheering loudly, hats and papers flying in the air throughout the bus. Thinking it better to have the traffic experts handle this complaint I radioed the State Police and waited for them to arrive. Enough close calls for one day.

When a Plan Comes Together

The evening was, clear, crisp and cold, with a full moon. It was the night before that religious holiday, rifle deer season. The radio call from station 89 in Stephenson summoned me from the Finlander cemetery east of Talbot where I had been patrolling for shiners. Four men dressed in outdoor gear, eager to speak with a conservation officer awaited my arrival in the lobby of the State Police post. The foursome had checked in at the town's only motel late that afternoon and felt compelled to report an incident they had just witnessed.

One hunter introducing himself as Dan stood and shook my hand. "We were just leaving to get some supper downtown when three guys came out of the room next to us. One of them had a 30-30 lever action rifle. No gun case. He stood by the right side of the car and put several shells in the gun, then got into the back seat. The other two got into the front and they drove off. We think they're going to do some poaching."

"I think you're right," I said. "Given the fact that they have a loaded rifle in the car puts them in violation already. Did you see which way they went?"

"They headed north up U S 41," said Dan. "It's a gray 1983 Chevy Caprice. Here's the license number." Dan handed me a scrap of paper with the license number of the vehicle.

"You guys are good, I'll give you that," I exclaimed. Far too often we get complaints describing the many sins of the miscreants, with not one shred of useful information as to who the perpetrators were, what they looked like, what they were driving, or even what direction they were headed.

Thanking the hunters I began the process of identifying the owner of the suspect vehicle. The license plate information revealed the owner of the car to be a resident of Manistique. With this information VCO Pete and I began our county wide search for the poachers.

At midnight we had not located the Caprice, and had not stopped any deer shiners. In the interest of having an early start on patrol the next morning we decided to forego the search and get some sleep. Our three illegal hunters had more than likely gone out to hunt under the cover of darkness and any deer they might have killed would be concealed, to be picked up the next day and 'legally' tagged. Hopefully this would be witnessed by someone and reported.

The report was not long in coming. Dawn had barely broken when the phone rang. It was Wendell Schiske, a farmer who lived on highway 577 west of Daggett. "Wayne, I was in my blind on the edge of the field along 577. This gray Chevy slows down and stops. Two guys get out and run into the field. Then they grab a dead doe that I didn't even know was there and ran to the car with it. They threw it in the trunk and took off to the north just as I was running up to them. I did get the license number."

The license plate number was the same as that of our mysterious Caprice from the night before. Now we had an illegal deer. Calling the resident conservation officer in Manistique I advised him that at some point during the day the gray Chevrolet would more than likely be cruising into his town. Armed with the case information, name and address of the vehicle owner, CO John agreed to set up some surveillance around the residence of the suspect. I would be watching for the vehicle throughout the county and stop at the motel to see if they had checked out.

The suspect trio had indeed checked out of the motel, so now it was a game to see who would catch the poachers first.

At 5:00 PM station 89 called instructing me to telephone CO John in Manistique. It seems that by the time our gray Chevy pulled in at the owner's residence, CO John had the State police, County Sheriff, two other CO's, and a U S Fish and Wildlife officer ready to pounce from all directions at once. The only one's missing were the coast guard, and they were probably watching for them at the harbor. The law breakers never had a chance to get out of the car before the army of law enforcement officers pounced. Two stiff, cold untagged does and one completely boned out deer of undetermined sex were in the trunk of the car. Our three poachers would be paying stiff fines, spend some time in jail, and not hunting for a good, long time.

A bookend finish to this deer season came after sunset on November 30, the last day for rifle deer hunting.

While enjoying supper with VCO Wade at the Village Inn we were approached by an excited patron who claimed to have overheard a most interesting conversation only minutes before. He had been sitting near several hunters from Canada who were grousing about the scarcity of deer in the area they had been hunting. Our informant stated that from the smell of things it was more than likely an alcohol problem than the absence of game that caused their lack of success. Before leaving the restaurant one of the Canadian group said "Well, that's okay. That farmer won't be renting out *that* camp until he does some serious fixing!" Apparently the disgruntled hunters had vandalized the farmer's hunting camp and departed without paying for their stay. Another mistake was their mentioning the name of the farmer. VCO Wade and I raced up U S 41 as far as the village of Carney without overtaking the Canadian van and trailer described by our informant.

Calling one of the Escanaba based CO's I described the Canadian vehicle, complete with license plate number supplied by the informant, and advised that I would immediately check on the condition of the farmer's hunting camp.

A fast ride out to the farmer's residence found him coming from the barn, having completed the milking of some 125 cows. When asked if he had rented his camp to a group of Canadian hunters he stated that he had indeed, and that they were due to leave soon. To my suggestion that they had already departed and in the process had vandalized his camp Farmer Ron expressed wide eyed surprise and agreed that we should check the camp for damage.

The camp was seriously damaged to say the least. The thick pane of the front picture window had been shot through with a small caliber rifle, as had several smaller side windows. Spaghetti sauce had been poured on the beds, and numerous holes had been punched in the walls. A vehicle had spun several 'donuts' in the lawn and beer cans littered the landscape. Time to get back with the officers up north. Word came back that a road block was being set up at Garden Corners, west of Manistique.

Within the hour the Escanaba officers reported the capture of the Canadian group at Garden Corners. Not only did they admit to vandalizing the farmer's camp, they turned over several illegal ducks they had shot and agreed to pay the fish and game violation fines and the farmer for the rental of the camp as well as to make financial compensation for the damage done to his building. This agreement came in lieu of being charged with the felony of defrauding an inn keeper. The guilty parties were released after forfeiting a generous amount suggested by the farmer and posting bond.

Back at the residence we received the heartfelt thanks from the farmer. "I have no idea how you knew the camp had been damaged, even before I knew the guys were gone," said Ron. "But I sure do appreciate your help."

"That's what happens when you have good information," I said. "I wish all cases could go this effortlessly."

The previous two cases occurred during the same deer season. In a movie or on television the scripted stories would make it seem that cases like these happen every day. In fact it is quite rare that the officer is in the right place at the right time, that the witnesses see just the right events, and that enough useful information is obtained to make a case. On the rare occasions that it does happen, we have the pleasure of saying "I LOVE IT when a plan comes together!"

Turn Turtle

During the winter months many of the boats that navigate the Great Lakes are pulled out of the water or into a sheltered boat slip, winterized, and stored throughout the freezing weather. Those that remain in service are given special care to see that the engines blocks do not freeze and burst, and that the hulls of the vessels are not damaged by freezing, crushing ice.

Motors are drained after each use, anti-freeze is introduced into the cooling systems and "bubblers" are placed around water bound vessels to create currents that surround the boats and prevent overnight freezing.

During the winter of 1998 the vessel PB-4 was moored at the Rogers City harbor which normally remains open during the winter. Currents from Lake Huron circulate through the harbor, preventing the formation of ice in the main channels. PB-4 was moored along the inside of the east break wall, allowing her to start up and put out on patrol at a moment's notice. RV anti- freeze kept the water circulating throughout the cooling system and an engine block heater ensured that the 671 Detroit diesel engine would start in any weather.

One of the problems unique to winter navigation in fresh water is the formation of ice on the hulls and superstructures of boats as spray from oncoming waves coat the vessel. If the ice builds to a significant thickness, the excess weight can cause the boat to become excessively top heavy and "turn turtle", rolling upside down, trapping the passengers inside. At times when an oncoming gale force wind catches a vessel by surprise passengers are obliged to go out on the slippery, ice covered deck and roof to chip off the forming ice with spuds, axes, or any other handy device. This situation is frightening, cold and not easily forgotten.

A New Year's Eve storm from the northeast buffeted the Rogers City harbor with eight to twelve foot waves. Gale force winds sent plumes of spray over the harbor wall, covering the walkway and PB-4 with lake water. Ice rapidly formed on the walk and boat in the frigid temperatures. Driving down to the harbor to check the boat I noticed the ice buildup and made a mental note to come down and de-ice the boat after the storm.

New Year's morning should be one morning of the year when a man is allowed to sleep in. But they have those dad blasted telephones in Rogers City too, and mine jangled me awake before the sun peered over the rosy southeastern horizon. It was Jeff, the harbor master.

"Wayne! You'd better get down to the harbor right now! Your boat is about to turn turtle!"

Stricken with anxiety I jumped from the bed and hastily donned insulated work clothes. The streets were a skating rink as I negotiated the slush coated streets, not yet plowed by the city boys. Should have taken time to make some coffee...

PB-4 was a sad sight indeed. Heeling hard to port she was coated in at least a foot of ice overall and threatening to roll over at any second. The only saving feature was a sheet of ice on the harbor surface, surrounding the vessel with an apron less than a foot thick. Frozen to the hull and extending out into the harbor for ten feet, the ice served as an outrigger and kept the boat upright.

Gingerly I crept down the ice covered walkway to PB-4. Ice sheeted the walk in a wedge shaped configuration, starting at the outside wall with a depth of three feet, slanting towards the water to a foot thick overhang on the inside of the harbor wall. Ice cleats would have been an asset, but in my excitement I had forgotten to dig them from one of the many still unpacked boxes that lined the walls of our most recent home. Slipping and sliding I reached the boat and jumped aboard.

I would never have thought that the weight of a single game warden could affect the balance of a vessel weighing more than fifty tons. Concluding my slide onto the deck at the port side of PB-4 I felt the slow list as she began to turn over towards the inside of the harbor. Jumping to the starboard rail I was relieved to see the boat return to an approximation of an upright position. Any move I made caused the boat to list, one way or the other. As the previous captain of this vessel, Arnie, once said "I didn't know which cheek of my butt to put the weight on!" I slowly leaned over and grasped the power box on the walkway and eased myself off the deck.

Rushing to the nearest telephone I called Grant, a builder and friend who would possess an electric jack hammer and would know others who would have more.

"Grant," I said. "I have to get several jack hammers. PB-4 is covered with a foot of ice and about to capsize. Can I borrow yours?"

"Absolutely, come right up and get it," said Grant. He also gave the numbers of two rental companies who would rent more hammers.

Next I called our District Supervisor Lou. One would think that at ten in the morning a body would at least be out of bed.

Oh yeah, this was New Year's Day. Sorry about that, but this was an emergency.

"Lou, PB-4 is ice covered and about to sink. Can you send as many CO's as possible to chop her off?" I asked.

"You know this is a holiday, don't you?" said Lou. "The overtime would kill our budget."

"How about we use some of that "scheduled overtime" we get each quarter," I said. "If the boat rolls over we're going to lose all the electronic equipment as well as having a bad oil spill right in the harbor."

"You have a point," said Lou. "I'll send some personnel, while you search for some jack hammers."

By noon we were gathered at the harbor. Those of us with ice cleats carefully plugged two jack hammers into the harbor power outlets and began to chip ice from the deck, starting with the port side. This was a most nervous time with the boat threatening to capsize several times, requiring those without hammers to stand on the starboard rail while we hammered away on the port side deck. Eventually PB-4 stabilized and all personnel were able to commence working on the ice.

Soon the engine hatch was cleared and two fuel oil heaters, known as "salamanders" were placed below the deck to warm the hull and assist in removing the ice from the sides of the craft. Remarkably the power cable to the engine heater was still intact and the motor was started to further supply heat to the interior of the boat. Our two crazy marine safety officers launched the lifeboat from the deck of PB-4 and floated around the boat, cracking sheets of ice from the hull.

At five PM the boat was cleared of ice and PB-4 rested proudly afloat, moved to the safety of the harbor's interior. Time for thanks all around, supper at Kortman's diner, and the reassurance that all would receive a day's overtime pay.

As we departed the diner to our vehicles, Anna, the CO

from Cheboygan walked over to my patrol car. "Next time, could you pick a better day?" she asked.

"What was wrong with today? You got eight hours of over-time," I said.

"Well now think about it. Last night was New Year's Eve. We were all celebrating. Do you have any idea what those jack hammers did to our already aching heads?!"

Snookered Again

The morning sun slowly broke over the southeastern horizon, spreading a welcome warm glow over the sleepy household. Shawn and Becky had already awakened and boarded the school bus while I slept off the fatigue of last night's patrol. Without looking out the window across the frozen, snow covered January fields one could easily imagine it to be the dawning of a pleasant summer's day. Of course I knew better and planned to spend a few more minutes in the warm bed, just enjoying the sleepy peace and quiet. My feet were warm and dry. I appreciated this, having spent much of my career thus far slogging around in wet, cold boots.

My peaceful reverie was rudely interrupted by the jangling of that darned phone. Morning phone calls almost always meant "Get out there and work!" I usually relished this opportunity. At the moment however I answered it with something less than enthusiasm. This call was going to interrupt me. Me with my warm, dry feet.

"Good morning," I said into the strangely shaped handset

of Kathy's Princess phone.

"Officer Coleman?" began the hesitant voice of an obvious first time caller.

"Please, call me Wayne," I said. "Others call me much worse."

"Well, this is Sandy Pike. I live south of you on Jimtown Road. Right at the intersection where Jimtown meets Hayward Lake Road there's a wounded Turkey. I saw it when I drove through with the bus just a few minutes ago."

I had met Sandy Pike only briefly several weeks before at a township fire-fighters meeting. She appeared to have been raised on a farm, a sort of Tomboy, able to handle most situations with confidence. Her mini farm harbored a horse and a few chickens, along with a large garden that supplemented her income from driving school bus. As a single mom, raising her three children must have been a challenge, to say the least.

"Is it still alive?" I asked.

"I saw feathers and blood on the side of the road where a car must have hit it. You can see where it dragged itself off into the swamp. I just can't stand the thought of that poor thing off in the woods, suffering. Can you come down and help me find it?" Sandy implored.

"Sure, I'll be right down," I said, rolling from the warm sheets. "Just give me a few minutes."

"Thank you so much," Said Sandy. "I'll meet you at the intersection."

Normally I would not have given this much attention to a wounded Wild Turkey. They were often killed along the county roads by vehicles. This situation was different in that it offered an opportunity to serve a concerned citizen who would likely report incidents of a more serious nature in the future if her call for help today were answered. The Turkey might have been a victim of poachers as well.

The thermometer hovered at ten degrees as I pulled in behind Sandy's blue Suburban along the short section of Hayward Lake road.

On the south side of the road Turkey feathers and blood were in abundance indicating an obvious car/Turkey collision. Drag marks extending southward into the Tamarack swamp indicated that the Turkey had struggled along atop the crusted snow, disappearing into the cranberry bog some hundred yards in the distance.

"Let's go, we can catch it!" exclaimed Sandy, eager for the chase. Little did she know how difficult waist deep, crusted snow can be to traverse.

"Okay, I'm game," I said "I'll break trail and you can follow."

The going was more than tough. It was insane. Hoping that travel through the bog might be somewhat easier on the frozen water I forged ahead.

I was wrong. Rotting vegetation in bogs often prevents freezing, even during extended periods of cold weather. Within the first few feet I had broken through the thin ice and was soaked with slimy mud to my knees. So much for the dry, warm feet. Within fifty yards of slogging through the mud we came to the end of the blood trail. It appeared that something, perhaps an Eagle, had taken the bird and flown away. Sandy had been following at a distance of a hundred feet, cheering my progress the whole time.

"Come on, Wayne! You can do it! Don't stop now!" shouted Sandy as I turned around to say that our quest had ended. At that moment a small flock of Ravens exploded from the bog fifty yards to the south, indicating the probable final resting place of our Turkey.

"I guess we might as well go have a look," I said. "We're not going to get any wetter than we already are."

The Turkey had been reduced by scavengers to no more than a partial skeleton. Satisfied that we had done everything we could, I turned to begin our arduous journey back to the highway.

"Hey, could I have one of the legs?" asked Sandy.

"Sure, why not," I said. Obviously Sandy just wanted a

chew toy for her dog. At least something could result from all this work. The leg easily separated from the carcass and we trudged back through the slushy mud to the road.

My uniform was drenched through with sweat and my boots were sodden with good old Hayward Lake boot suckin' mud as I bid Sandy good day, thanking her for the call. The next hour was spent in the sauna as the steam chased away a case of the chills.

The next time Sandy called I was typing reports and was happy for the interruption when the phone rang. Winter had turned to early spring and I was suffering from "Cabin fever". Conditions were too warm for ice fishing patrol, but too early for fish runs. I would welcome any diversion.

"Wayne," Sandy began, "I've got another Turkey deal. No more frogging around in the swamp, but my neighbor has a Turkey eating the feed she puts out for the chickens. It won't leave the yard and it chases her whenever she leaves the house."

Every now and then a Turkey will go rogue. It might be a young Tom that has been shunned by the flock. For numerous reasons, occasionally a single Turkey will show up at some-one's residence demanding to be fed and bullying the domestic animals. Capturing and moving these pests can often be quite a challenge. Loading up a large cardboard box and a short piece of gill net I headed for Sandy's farm.

Sandy offered a cup of coffee when I arrived and as she brought out the cups I noticed a number of pictures and tro-phies on her living room wall. Suddenly I stopped short. There on a beautifully varnished plaque was "the Turkey leg"! It had been mounted on the plaque with the leg extending horizontally and the foot curled into a fist. Except for the middle talon, which was extended straight up, forming that universal sign known as "flipping the bird".

Pointing to the plaque I said to Sandy "Explain this."

Sandy giggled. "Yeah, The U P Salute! It's really for my neighbor down the road. I'm going to give it to her for her birthday, but I'm enjoying it for now."

"You mean you snookered me into all that work so you could get a Turkey leg? I could have found one a lot easier that that!"

Sandy's face reddened. "I'm sorry, but it was kind of fun, hey?"

"Well, I guess it was, looking back on it," I said, finishing the coffee. "Let's get over to your neighbor's house and capture that bird." Reaching to open the kitchen door I noticed an old single shot 22 rifle standing in the corner. All the locals had one; varmints were common.

Anna Carlson was the typical Upper Peninsula Swedish grandmother, beautifully embroidered kitchen apron, wire rimmed glasses, small bun hair style and all.

Leading the way around her small garage she pointed to a large, defiant, bearded Turkey. The bird glared in our direction as if to say "Well, what are you going to do about it?" The young tom must have weighed fifteen pounds and would have been a match for the average farm dog. This was going to be fun.

Unrolling the gill net I fastened it across the span of twenty feet or so between the house and garage in an upright position, resembling a large volleyball net. Normally a Turkey when chased toward the net will not see the monofilament mesh and become entangled, lending itself to capture. While Sandy and I were able to herd the Turkey into the net, the meshes easily broke from the sheer power of the bird and it ran free. Another plan would have to be devised.

Several days of brainstorming yielded little other than perhaps leaving Anna's garage door open and enticing the Turkey in with food, closing the door and catching the bird in the enclosed building. While enroute to Menominee I stopped by Anna's house to tell her of the plan.

When Anna answered her door I was immediately enveloped by the delicious odor of cooking meat, spices, dressing, gravy; simply heaven to smell. Obviously someone was planning a superb dinner. I began to tell Anna of my plan when she held up her hand, pausing me mid-sentence.

"Oh, you don't need to worry about that any more. That Turkey is gone and I don't think he'll be back," said Anna.

"What made it leave, and how do you know it will stay gone?" I asked.

"Oh, I just have a feeling," said Anna. "Thank you for all the help. You've been so nice!"

"That's what we do, Ma'am. Just call any time you need help. It smells like you're going to put on quite a dinner."

"Yes indeed I am. I'm having Sandy and the kids over for supper. She's so nice. Always there to help when you need it," said Anna.

Once underway to Menominee I began to ponder the recent curious situation. The turkey is gone and won't be back. The house smells like cooking for a holiday. What holiday? I think maybe Thanksgiving. Thanksgiving in March? But yes, that smelled like a Turkey cooking. Anna said that Sandy is always there to help. Sandy has a 22 rifle behind her door, and I bet she knows how to use it. And she will be taking her kids to Anna's for a Turkey dinner.

Of course nothing could be proven unless someone confessed to killing the Turkey. Sometimes things are better left not investigated. I was sure that none of these good souls would ever break the law. And besides, people are allowed to protect their property. Yeah! That's what it could be; a sort of self-defense. If it really happened. Dang, I hate these arguments in my head. Even worse I hate being "Snookered again"!

Trail Rage

"Bam-bam-bam-bam!...bam-bam-bam-bam!" It was that reoccurring dream again. I was back in Vietnam, on guard duty. I was back on tower sixteen, searching out into the black night of the free fire zone that surrounded our compound. Above me 'Lucky John', our fifty caliber machine gun spit out half inch pieces of copper jacketed lead into the brush where our unseen enemy lurked. "Bam-bam-bam-bam!" The explosions were ear shattering, but we were grateful for anything that would keep the Vietcong at bay.

"Bam-bam-bam-bam!...bam-bam-bam-bam!". I opened my eyes. Cold gray light from the overcast late November morning filtered through the curtains of the bedroom window. The alarm clock on the nightstand read 7:30 AM, indicating that I had been asleep for only three hours since the end of my patrol.

"Bam-bam-bam-bam!.....bam-bam-bam-bam!" The explosions persisted even though I was awake. With this I realized that someone was pounding at the front door, insisting that I answer. Hastily I pulled on some sweat pants and rushed downstairs to greet whatever incident that might cause such a relentless need for attention.

Ashen faced, shaking visibly and sweating profusely in the twenty degree chill the bright orange clad individual who greeted me was in obvious pain. Leaning on the porch railing for support, his breath came in short gasps as he said weakly "I've just been run over!"

Placing his arm around my shoulder I ushered him into the living room and asked him to sit in the closest chair. After several moments the hunter's composure improved and he was able to relate the previous events of the morning that brought him to my door step.

"I was hunting on Charlie Walter's property just two miles west of here. Just after daybreak I shot at a doe across that narrow field. She was off to the east, down in the edge of the swamp. She ran off and I don't think I hit her.

"A few minutes after that I heard Ray Townsend, my neighbor to the west start his pickup and drive off to the south towards his camp. We don't get along and I try to stay away from him as much as possible. About five minutes later he drove around the block into Charlie's property and came up the trail that crosses the field at an angle towards my blind.

"I walked out to meet him but he drove right past me, and he was swearing at me out the window as he passed by. Then he drove on up around my bait pile and headed back right towards me. I was standing just off to the side of the trail and I jumped to the side, but he swerved right at me and hit me in the left leg. I was knocked to the ground and couldn't get up for several minutes. I was sure that my leg was broken, but after a few minutes I found I could get up and walk a little."

"Did he give the nature of his complaint?" I asked. "It sounds pretty serious to me."

"Not a word, other than a lot of swearing and name calling." After he knocked me down he just drove off. Didn't come back to check on me or anything."

Under normal circumstances an incident of this nature would be turned over to a law enforcement entity whose experience included motor vehicle violations and assaults on a daily basis. Calls to the Michigan State police and Sheriff's department revealed that neither agency had an officer available to investigate the complaint. The serious nature of the affair demanded that action be taken immediately. This would be my case, like it or not.

"Let's get you some help," I said. "You need to see a doctor right away. Let me call the rescue squad."

"No, no. I'm on my way to the hospital right now. I can make it just fine," said the victim.

"Well, let me get some information. I'll need your name, address, date of birth and some means of contacting you," I advised. "I'll be investigating this incident and it looks like I'll probably be arresting your neighbor for assault. If you don't mind I'll have to take a few pictures of your injury."

Howard Higgins, as identified by his driver's license, pulled down his hunting pants to reveal a huge, ugly blue-gray bruise on the outer side of his left thigh. Swelling had increased the limb to nearly twice its normal size. While the bone was obviously not broken it was definitely an injury of a serious nature. Mr. Higgins limped out to his pickup and was off to the emergency room for X-rays and evaluation. Putting on a uniform I set off to the Townsend camp.

Ray Townsend was a seasonal resident from Ann Arbor whose self-employed status allowed him to spend a great deal of time at his Menominee county hunting camp. It was said that his abrasive personality often made it difficult for adjoining landowners to get along during normal neighborly activities such as agreement over property lines and the repair of the fences that defined their boundaries. His camp was located at the end of a short county road that extended into the center of a section of private land, making for a very private, isolated retreat. Pulling up at the camp I was met by Mr. Townsend who was at the patrol car door before I had completely stopped.

"Who gave you permission to come in here?" he shouted.

"Can't you read the 'No trespassing' signs?"

"Just calm down and listen," I said, getting out of the patrol car. "I'm investigating an incident that happened up in Charlie Walter's field with one of his hunters. It seems that you were involved. Just listen while I advise you of your Miranda rights."

Ray stood quietly while being advised of his rights under the Miranda decision, nodding his head when asked if he understood them. "Now Ray, knowing your rights, would you be willing to tell me what happened?" I asked.

Ray wasted no time. "That idiot has been shooting at everything that moves all day long since the season began. He shoots does, fawns, button bucks, and it ruins my hunting. He's got a big pile of bait up there and he's cutting off my deer! How can I get anything with him scaring all of my deer away?"

"That's something that you both need to settle as neighbors," I said. "What I need to know is what went on earlier this morning when you drove up through Charlie's field to Mr. Higgins's deer blind."

"I just drove in there, that's all," said Ray. "I just wanted to look at his bait pile."

"Did you make contact with Mr. Higgins?" I asked. "I was told that you struck him with your pickup truck."

"He wouldn't get out of the way!" exclaimed Mr. Townsend, becoming increasingly agitated. "Jumped right into the path of my truck. He wasn't hurt. I didn't even touch him!"

"Okay, we'll be investigating that further," I said, walking around Mr. Townsend's light green half ton pickup. The left front fender sported what appeared to be a fresh 'oilcan' type of dent; the type which can be pushed back out by hand, but still leaves a slight wrinkle in the surface of the paint. "I'll need to see your identification as well."

"I'm not showing you anything!" shouted Mr. Townsend. "You know who I am. Unless you have a warrant, I want you to leave, now!"

I wasn't about to argue the legal points of investigating a felony with Ray Townsend. The license plate on his pickup would give all the information needed. I was happy to leave his unpleasant company and depart for the Walters farm.

The field where the assault had taken place was knee deep in green alfalfa hay, several hundred yards wide, extending southward from the gravel road for a quarter of a mile. A two track trail ran diagonally across the field to a deer blind at the top of a hill midway down the west side. Walking the trail I could see where a vehicle had recently driven up to the blind and around a pile of carrots fifty yards or so into the field to the east of the blind. At one point some fifty yards toward the road it was evident that the vehicle had swerved off the trail, making a sweep to the west for about fifty feet. Someone or something appeared to have fallen just to the west of the swerve tracks and rolled around in the alfalfa, flattening a small patch of the crop. The swerving tracks turned back to the trail without any type of disturbance that might indicate that the vehicle had stopped. The account given by Mr. Higgins was by far the most believable.

Several hours were spent typing the police report during which Mr. Higgins telephoned with the results of his X-rays. While his leg was not broken, several hairline fractures made it necessary for him to use crutches for the next six weeks. Upon learning that I would be filing charges for the assault, Howard stated that he would be happy to testify to the facts in court, should the need arise.

A visit to the Prosecuting Attorney later that day resulted in warrants for assault with intent to do great bodily harm, leaving the scene of an accident and recreational trespass. Accompanying me on the return trip to Stephenson was Sheriff's detective Grant

Norris. Our destination: the Townsend camp. By now it was after sunset, and about time to wrap things up for the day.

The greeting of "Come on in," would have been different had Ray Townsend known who was knocking; but then again we weren't there to ask permission to enter. Ray jumped to his feet upon seeing Grant and I in the doorway and his face was a mask of surprise and anger. His eyes darted to the deer rifle standing in the corner several feet to his right.

"Ray, calm down. Don't even think about the gun. Turn around with your hands behind your back." Ray was hand-cuffed without further incident and advised of the charges against him.

Mr. Townsend was transported to the Menominee county jail and booked in, to be released on bond several hours later. Mr. Townsend was able to plead to the lesser charge of assault with a motor vehicle and spent some time in jail. His driver's license was revoked for one year; a crippling penalty for someone in his position.

No good reason was ever given for Ray Townsend's violent anger and actions toward Mr. Higgins, except that Howard seemed to have interfered with Ray's hunting in some manner. All the pain and suffering on both sides could have easily been avoided by working things out together before deer season as good neighbors should. Since the disposition of the case I have had no contact with either gentleman, but I still hope that they were somehow able to reconcile their differences and put this case of 'trail rage' behind them.

Those Embarrassing Moments

W e've all had them. Those moments, however brief, that make us wish that we were someone else, somewhere else, far, far, away. It may be something we have said or done, or sometimes something we haven't said or done that show us to be the fool in front of God and the whole, wide world. Those moments make us wish that there were a 'rewind' button for life, or at least a 'delete' button that would allow us to relive or re-say something that we can never take back, no matter how hard we try.

As a conservation officer I had no trouble experiencing embarrassing moments. Not only was I very adept at creating my own embarrassments; I was assisted by legions of good citizens who seemed to delight in exposing me for the fool that I was, in the most public forums possible. In my childhood I can remember my father describing a miscue or a misstatement as "Putting one's foot in one's mouth." At times it seemed that the only time I opened my mouth was to change feet. But enough of that. Many of my stories describe in great detail my embarrassing experiences as an officer of the law. A few of them will be mentioned here, but this story will center largely on the embarrassing situations brought upon good people by themselves, as a result of just being themselves, and the burdens imposed upon them by human nature in general. With this in mind, please forgive me if I keep the mention of names, both real and fictitious, to a minimum.

In the year 1977, just prior to my transfer from State Parks to Law Enforcement division I spent considerable time with the assistant manager of Traverse City State Park. He was an imposing figure of a man, at least six foot eight inches in stature, and was quite self-conscious about his height. During one of our visits he related the following two experiences to me:

It was a beautiful spring evening in Traverse City. The cherry blossoms were out in their full fragrant beauty and the warm, sunny afternoon made for ideal conditions to ask one's bride to be out to supper at the Cherry Berry Supper club, which my friend did. Upon finishing a delicious seafood dinner my friend visited the men's room. Upon washing his hands he was obliged because of his height to bend over to see himself in the mirror as he combed his hair. Being conscious of his height he felt it necessary to make some sort of explanatory remark upon hearing the bathroom door open, signaling the entrance of another person.

"Man, they must design these mirrors for *midgets*", my friend remarked.

Imagine his chagrin as he turned to meet a smiling dwarf, all of four feet tall.

"Don't give it a thought," said the diminutive man with a laugh. "I hear this type of thing all the time." While somewhat reassuring, it did not diminish my friend's embarrassment.

My friend had yet another bout with 'hoof in mouth disease' while on duty. It seems that a camper had locked his keys in his pickup truck and came to the park office for assistance.

Recent policy forbade State employees from rendering assistance in the form of 'breaking' into cars, and it was necessary to recommend the services of a local locksmith. The locksmith was summoned and soon access was gained to the vehicle. Upon successful completion of the service call the camper returned to the park office to thank my friend for his assistance. The camper mentioned that the service call had cost fifty dollars.

"Yeah, those guys usually charge you an arm and a leg," said my friend offhandedly. It was then that he noticed the camper's prosthetic right arm. Jabbering like a magpie to divert the conversation somewhere; *anywhere* besides the absence of limbs, my friend said that he covered most of the topics found in the Encyclopedia in the next five minutes, but still had a red face.

During my tenure as a conservation officer I encountered many good people in embarrassing situations. Usually the best way to handle the situation was to act as if I didn't witness anything out of the ordinary. For instance, young, attractive ladies canoe remote stretches of the Menominee River topless every day of the week. Usually my partners and I could pull off the nonchalance effectively, but sometimes things just got too intense, too funny, or too crazy to be ignored. Of those things, memories are made.

One late night as I returned home from deer shiner patrol my eye caught a glint of reflected chrome a short distance down a dead end side road. This could mean several things; a broken down vehicle, a hidden car used by burglars, a rape, a kidnapping, a fish or game violation. As we often said in the trade, not much good happens after midnight.

Driving down the highway a half mile I doused the headlights, turned around and returned with lights out, turning down the dead end road and speeding up to the parked car.

Turning on the headlights and jumping from the car I was greeted by two totally naked people in the front seat of a sedan. This young man and lady were taking part in a long abandoned ritual known as 'parking'. Many years ago when automobiles were known to have spacious front and rear seats, teen age couples would travel to remote areas, park the car and proceed to show their affection to each other for several hours until it was time to go home. (Not that I myself ever participated in any such activity, to any great extent. I just remember people talking about it, that's all. C'mon now, you gotta trust me. Would a government agent ever lie to you?) Anyway, be that as it may, this fellow and girl had not picked up on the off season purpose of the hunting camp, and were very surprised to see an officer of the law at their car window. They might have tried to put on some items of clothing, had they all not been scattered in disarray about the back seat. All they could do was giggle nervously and wonder what this crazy game warden would do next.

"Okay, well, listen here," I stammered. "I just need to know that the lady is here voluntarily, and isn't being abducted. Are you okay, ma'am? Now's your time to speak up."

"Sure, I'm fine," said the girl.

"Okay, I'm outta here," I said, making a swift departure.

This would not have earned mention in this story, had it not been for the fact that I kept encountering this naked couple several times during the ensuing weeks. We always seemed to end up at the same location at the same time. After the fourth encounter I had seen enough, both figuratively and realistically.

"Look," I finally said. "We have to stop meeting like this. Go half a mile west and half a mile south. You'll see a big barn on the left. Turn left onto that gravel road and go a quarter mile east. There is a long driveway to the south where no one ever goes. You'll be safe there."

The driver thanked me, and that was the last that I ever saw of him. Thankfully.

When it comes to fishing, the Big Cedar River wins the turkey. More violations take place on that poor, beleaguered river than anywhere else I can name. Perhaps the remoteness of the stream inspires confidence in the less than scrupulous, and thus makes it a Game Warden's favorite hunting ground.

One bright, summer morning I followed my instincts and traveled to a seldom patrolled region of the county known as the Jam Dam area. This farming community is known for its hardworking, honest, neighborly residents. As such it is no surprise that law enforcement entities see little need to concentrate their efforts in this locale, knowing that about the only thing the officer on patrol will encounter are friendly, helpful citizens. By the same token it is common for residents of this community to adopt a somewhat cavalier attitude when it comes to following the fish and game laws. No one is breathing down their neck about having a hunting or fishing license, so it must not be that big a deal. Does that buck have horns just a shade under three inches? Not that big a deal. And so it goes. The old catch 22 of law enforcement.

The bright sun flitted through the springtime trees, and the warm breeze drifting through the driver's window was making it most difficult to imagine myself as a responsible servant of the public. The urge to just pull off on a side road and take a short nap was nearly overpowering. I turned left on the next available side road, knowing that I would soon be in the area of the Four Corners. Within a half mile I crossed the Big Cedar River on a recently rebuilt bridge. Two vehicles, an old sedan and a farm pickup were parked on the northwest shoulder of the bridge; a sure sign that local fishermen lurked in the shade of this river crossing. I would definitely have to check this out, if for no other reason than to return to some state of wakefulness.

I parked the patrol car a hundred yards west of the bridge so as not to make anyone aware of my approach. Upon nearing the bridge I could hear an animated conversation taking place below.

"Okay, good deal. I'll go get a bucket."

"I don't know dad. It looks kinda small."

By this time I was under the bridge. Before me stood two young men in their teens at the water's edge. One of them held a Small mouth Bass, nearly big enough to legally keep, but obviously undersized. Between us walked a man in his late thirties, probably the father of one or both of the youths. As the man walked, he turned back to face the two, talking to them while approaching me, slowly turning in my direction.

"I don't know, but I've fished this river for thirty years, and I never once worried about the legal sizes of fis...."

At this he turned to face me, the one he had never before faced in his thirty years of fishing this river. His imitation of Porky Pig was immediate. He stammered. He stuttered. Only when I held up my hand did he cease his embarrassed, failed attempt at explaining himself. I let his son settle the situation. Out of the mouths of babes...

"Yeah, good shot, dad," said his son, and we all laughed nervously. The small fish was released and I left the scene without checking any licenses, confident that all necessary lessons had been learned.

Another time and another place on the Big Cedar River found Paul, my partner to the north and me hiding and watching Salmon fishermen at the Cedar River access site. The cold late October weather had brought the Salmon into the river mouth with a vengeance, and anglers from as far away as Chicago were clamoring for the chance to hook one of those Great Lakes trophies. Of late most of the nighttime fishermen consisted of those less than sportsmanlike; those who would seek their reward by snagging, rather than enticing the fish to bite of their own volition. One fisherman, a huge specimen of a man, seemed to be in command of the limelight, both physically and vociferously. His loud vocalizations as well as his 'hogging' of the entire launch area by casting across the lines of other fishermen soon resulted in his having most of the fishable shoreline to himself. Soon he had foul hooked a large Salmon; a fact that he made loudly and abundantly clear to all within earshot.

"There boys!" he would exclaim. "I told you I'd get you into some fish! This pays for it all! This pays for the whole trip!"

This went on for most of an hour as our large friend battled the snagged Salmon. Paul and I found it difficult to continue our concealment, fighting the urge to laugh out loud as the poacher continued to exclaim "This pays for it all you guys! This pays for the whole trip, right here!"

At long last the huge Salmon began to tire and the fish was brought to shore. Upon clearing the water line the fish was immediately tackled by Paul and myself, not wanting to lose this piece of evidence. As we both jumped from our places of concealment and pounced upon the fish, several camera flashes lit the night scene. Somewhere out there is a photo of a large Salmon with two Conservation Officers in mid-air tackling the poor fish.

Once the surprise of our presence had subsided, identification of the snagger was made and a citation issued. Through ways which I will not explain, the snagger was able to keep the fish. It was the least I could do, knowing that never again could our large friend enter a Chicago bar frequented by his friends without the phrase "This pays for the whole trip!" being shouted, and a round of drinks bought by our snagging buddy.

At times even the violation as small as littering can be the cause of a moment of embarrassment. I had been working only one week when I discovered a fairly large amount of litter in the ditch along the county road just a mile north of my home. Charred remains of waste paper indicated that a 'burn barrel' had been emptied in the ditch, out of convenience, rather than by seeking a more appropriate though more difficult method of disposal, deeper into private land. One partially burned envelope gave the address of a resident just a quarter mile to the west.

Upon my knock I was greeted by a most cordial, grandmotherly lady. Her greeting of "Oh, you must be the new neighbor. Come on in!" was a bit disconcerting, given the nature of my visit. I immediately got down to the business at hand.

"Ma'am, I discovered a burn barrel dumped into the ditch just a quarter mile east of here."

"Oh," she exclaimed. "I don't know who could have done that."

"Well ma'am," I said, "the name on this envelope is your name."

"Why, it could have been us!" she exclaimed, as surprised as if I had just stepped off the moon. Being a brand new officer, I wasn't prepared to cope with such open honesty, nor such a display of honest embarrassment. Her youngest son saved the day.

"Hey man, that was me. Can you give me a break if I clean it up?" he shouted from across the room.

"You bet. Thank you very much," I said, and made my departure. Something about the mother's honest embarrassment told me that she did not deserve this, and I needed to just leave.

Another litterbug deserved everything he got, and then some. I had been working with a new recruit, teaching him the fine points of nighttime crime detection. With us that night was VCO Wade, who occupied the back seat of the patrol car. We had been watching the open, blalant antics of a particular deer shiner who had been flashing his beacon about the night sky in an obvious effort to be stopped by the Game Warden, should he be on patrol. Once the shiner's vehicle was in an open, safe area I activated the overhead flashing blue light and brought the shiner's car to a halt. As could be expected, four persons occupied the car, giving our shiner an audience.

"Oh yeah, we got a couple of machine guns, and a few does in the trunk," expounded the driver, obviously enjoying the fact that he had attracted the attention of the DNR. After the required cursory search, the shiner was sent on his way, knowing that he would be bragging to his friends about how he 'put one over' on the Game Warden by making me stop him.

But the story doesn't end there. Upon returning to the patrol car, recruit Vincente and I were informed by VCO Wade, who had been sitting in the patrol car, that when Vince and I had turned our backs, the shiner smirked broadly to his friends, wadded up a large, foil plastic potato chip bag and threw it into the ditch before re-entering his own car. Gee fellas, now we gotta go and enforce the law again...

The shiner's embarrassment and chagrin were evident as I issued the summons after stopping him for the second time. "Can't you give a guy a break?" he asked.

"Sure, if you'd littered by accident," I said. "This ticket merely reflects your bad attitude. Have fun living this one down."

Sometimes people just can't help themselves. If you're going to bad mouth an officer, make sure who it is you're bad mouthing him to. In the spirit of other agency co-operation I would sometimes assist the Sheriff's department or the Michigan State Police in their Marine or Off Road Vehicle safety programs. On One particular evening I was to speak at the Lake Township hall, concerning the new ordinance that allowed four wheelers to use the shoulder of county roads much the same as snowmobiles. Somehow the topic was changed to the nearly impassible springtime roads in the Oxbow area in south Lake Township. The comment was made that during certain times of the year, those roads were impassable by anything other than four wheelers. I advised that if only four wheelers could use those roads, I highly doubted that any law enforcement officers would be venturing into that area anyway. One individual was adamant.

"There's one DNR officer who will get you, no matter what. If you're breaking the law, He'll get you."

Researching my memory I was finally able to remember him as a fellow who had parked his unlicensed pickup truck several hundred feet into the State forest north of the village of Banat. I had written him for unregistered ORV to save him the expense of unregistered, uninsured motor vehicle. Nonetheless he had to complained to the local sportsman's' clubs and to the Lansing office; pretty much getting laughed out of both institutions. Now he was sitting in the meeting, saying that the local DNR officer was going to get you, no matter what. At this particular meeting I was in civilian clothes, but thought that everyone, after 24 years, knew who I was.

"Well," I said. "I just don't see anybody in the law enforcement community coming down there to issue citations if they can't drive there."

"You don't know this guy," he said. "He's been known to lie on a river bottom and breathe through a straw just to catch fishermen without a license!"

At this the meeting pretty much adjourned. I was told that later, across the street at the Camp Shakey Saloon our friend was teased mercilessly from meeting attendees who were more than happy to enlighten our friend as to whom he was talking to, and about.

On another occasion I was cruising along just at dark with the headlights off. The beam of a flashlight in a farm field off to the right attracted my attention and I stopped to walk into the field and talk with what had to be archery hunters returning from their evening's hunt. Approaching the location of the flashlight I could hear the conversation of two individuals. One appeared doubtful, the other confident.

"I don't know," said the first. "I really think we should tag this."

"Hey, I know it's your first bow kill," said the second. "But let's not burn up your tag on something this small one. You may get a chance at a bigger one later."

"Yeah, but it just ain't legal," said the first.

"Listen pal," said the first. "Even if the DNR was standing right here, the worst he could do is make you tag the deer. Now let's get this back into camp and cut up. We'll eat it all this week."

In the darkness I fell into step with them. Within a hundred yards both hunters knew that something was amiss.

"Hey Pete, who's walking alongside us?" asked the first.

"Three guesses fellas," I said.

"Yep, yep!" said the second. "Just headed for the road where we'll be puttin' on the tag and heading back for camp!"

The hunter was allowed to tag his deer and issued a citation for failure to immediately tag his deer. Along with the advice that he could have been charged with possession of illegal deer came the embarrassment of being caught at his own game.

In the thirty some years of my serving the public, many more stories of this nature abound, but you get the point. I truly believe that God gave us all the capacity to be embarrassed for a reason. This aspect of our lives serves to occasionally jerk the carpet from under us, reminding us that we're all just human beings, none of us being perfect. Just think, when we finally reach that final day and meet our maker, our lives will pass in review. We'll get to relive all those moments again in the presence of the one who designed all of this. Sleep well, good and faithful reader.

The Telltale Bullet

Like many of my stories, this one begins with the jangling of that darned phone, interrupting me from a most enjoyable afternoon nap. Why does the phone always have to ring when I'm sleeping? Or is it that I'm sleeping a lot more than I realize, and the phone has taken on the responsibility of getting me back out to work, where good Game Wardens ought to be.

Be that as it may, the call was a good one, coming from Louie Grant in Cedar River.

"Wayne!" he began, "I don't know how to begin!"

Louie, a retired businessman from Chicago, was obviously in a high state of agitation. Something had upset him to the point that he was barely able to speak. "You already have Louie," I said. "Just start from the top and tell me what happened. I'll sort the wheat from the chaff as you talk."

"Well, I was bow hunting up in my tree stand off Bay Mills road. About three thirty I hear this car or truck out on the gravel road coming to a stop. The road is about fifty yards north of my blind. Then I heard two shots from a .22 rifle. Right away a doe runs in towards me and falls dead right under my tree blind. I hear a car door slam and pretty soon this guy comes in towards me, slowly tracking the deer, and it's Oscar Maskal!"

"You mean the Oscar Maskal that has the gas station right there in town?" I asked.

"One and the same. He grabbed the deer by the front feet and dragged it back out to the road and away they went. I'm so mad I could chew nails and spit rust!"

"Okay Louie, just stay where you are at home and I'll be right out."

The seven miles east to Cedar River were covered in record time. As the late October sun set into the cedar trees I pulled into Louie's cottage on Bay Mills road. Louie bounded from the front door and handed me a Styrofoam cup of black coffee. "Let's walk up the road and I'll show you where it all happened," he said, still in a state of high excitement.

Tracks were visible where a vehicle had stopped near a small clearing on the south side of the road bordering Louie's property. A search for spent rifle casings proved futile, as often happens when rifles are fired from a vehicle. The empty shells tend to land inside the cab rather than outside where their discovery would be most helpful in solving the case. Footprints along with a drag mark and small spots of blood told the story of someone having taken an animal the size of a deer from the woods beyond the clearing. Louie's blind was located approximately twenty yards inside the tree line in a thick cedar tree. Beneath the blind a blood stain indicated where the deer had fallen and died. To someone watching the scenario of a poacher retrieving a deer from twelve feet directly below, this would have been an exciting experience indeed.

"That deer should have been mine," lamented Louie. "No way should Oscar get away with this."

"Well Louie," I said, "we just have to be patient here and gather as much evidence as we can. Right now all we have is your word as to what went down. I believe you, but we'll probably have to convince a judge and jury."

At that moment a vehicle could be heard rattling up Bay Mills road. As Louie and I walked from the woods and began to cross the clearing toward the road Oscar Maskal pulled to a stop and stepped from his old yellow Chevrolet pickup. More than likely my driving past his business had alerted him to the possibility that I was on my way to this complaint. Trying to appear nonchalant he waved and gave a nervous smile.

"What's up, fellas?" he asked.

"You know what's up, you rat!" exclaimed Louie. "You shot my deer, and now you're gonna pay!" Louie's face had reddened and he visibly shook with anger.

"Chill out, you old fool." countered Oscar. "I shot that deer perfectly legal, with a bow, and you know it!"

Louie began a scathing retort and it was necessary to intervene, lest the situation turn violent. "Gentlemen, please!" I said. "Calm down and let's see how this all shakes out. This shouting will get you nowhere."

Oscar felt it necessary to have his story told, and he began. "I was on my way to the dump a couple of hours ago and I saw this here doe standing in that clearing. I stopped and left the engine running, snuck out the passenger's side of the truck, and shot her with my bow over the bed of the truck. I tracked her a little ways into Louie's woods and found her, tagged her and took her home."

"Yeah, you found her all right," snapped Louie. "You found her with that .22 rifle and she fell dead right below my tree stand. I saw the whole thing!"

"No way, you old coyote," Oscar retorted. "You're just mad because I shot it offa your land. I thought we were better neighbors than that."

Again it was necessary to separate the two verbal combatants while the conflict was still restricted to words.

"Listen Oscar," I said. "Give me a few minutes and I'll meet you at the gas station and I'll get your statement. We'll sort this all out and the truth will show up somewhere between the two stories."

I remained several minutes after Oscar departed, taking down more information. From the evidence available it appeared that the incident had occurred according to Louie's description. At this point evidence was somewhat sparse, however.

Arriving at Oscar's service station I was met by Oscar who handed me a broken, bloody hunting arrow.

"There, that's the arrow I shot that deer with," said Oscar. "You can see the blood all over it." The arrow was indeed covered with blood. Strangely the blood did not completely encircle the arrow as it would have had it passed through an animal. Added to this, the smear marks left by the blood did not travel along the shaft, but around it, as if the arrow had been rolled around upon some bloody object.

"Okay Oscar, let me take this arrow as evidence. If we end up in court, the jury will want to see this."

"No, I can't let you take it, it's mine," said Oscar. "If we go to court, I'll be the one to present it. If you want it, you'll have to get a warrant."

"No problem Oscar, as you wish. But let me see the deer," I said.

"The deer is all processed and up at camp," said Oscar. This in itself was suspicious. Normally a hunter tended to hang the deer for a week or so to age the meat. Deer that were immediately processed were always questionable.

"Well, at least let me see the hide. I'll be able to tell if the deer was hit by an arrow or a bullet by the entrance wound," I said.

"Funny thing about that," said Oscar with a sly smile. "While we were up there jawing with old man Grant, a fur buyer came through and bought the hide. You can ask my wife."

"You mean to tell me that in these last few hours of daylight you shot a deer, processed it, and sold the hide to a buyer who just happened to come by at the right moment?" I asked. "It sounds like a lot of convenient stuff happening awfully fast."

"I don't care what it sounds like to you," said Oscar. "That's my story and I'm sticking to it. Now unless you have a search warrant, I'd say that our business here is finished."

Driving south from Cedar River I knew that Oscar fully expected me to show up at his establishment and home with a search warrant, and he was right. Within the hour the assistant county prosecutor had been called into the court house from his supper and was in the process of typing out a warrant for the seizure of any and all firearms, home processed meat, and deer parts to be found on the Maskal property.

"Can't you ever come in for these warrants at a decent hour?" lamented Mike, the assistant prosecutor. "It's always a weekend or the middle of the night with you DNR guys."

"I'm working on it," I said. "As you can see I have them breaking the law at more reasonable times. This one's only at seven thirty at night."

"Well, tell them to shoot their deer on Monday mornings from now on," said Mike.

Nine PM found Sergeant Bart, two neighboring officers and myself at Oscar's doorstep, warrant in hand. Oscar was not surprised at our appearance, nor was he pleased.

"Just had to come back and disturb my whole family," said Oscar. "Well, come on in. You won't find anything."

Strangely, for the residence of an avid sportsman, Oscar's house and service station were completely devoid of any firearms or deer parts, with the exception of a neck roast and several tenderloin steaks, freshly packaged and placed in the freezer. One side of the tenderloin cuts showed fresh blood, as if cut by an arrow or bullet. We determined to take them to the crime lab to check for evidence of lead. As a matter of course we seized the neck roast as well, just to be thorough.

Presenting a validated deer tag, Oscar grinned broadly. "Here, you might as well take this with you. It proves that the deer was taken and tagged legally. "I told you that most of the meat and the hide were gone."

The next day the roast and steaks were delivered to the crime lab in Marquette to be processed for evidence of lead in the meat. My hopes of gleaning any helpful evidence were not high.

The prosecution for the illegal taking of deer proceeded on Louie's testimony alone. There was no doubt in my mind that the deer had been poached, and I felt that a fair minded jury would believe it as well. A warrant for Oscar's arrest was issued and served. A not guilty plea was entered by his attorney and a trial date was set.

Two weeks before the trial I was once again awakened by that gosh awful phone. Maybe it's the hours I work. Maybe I should get a job that I don't like so much, hey? It was the crime lab. I was ready for the disappointment of hearing that no lead was found in any of the meat when the technician began with a sentence that brought me out of bed like a rocket, nearly knocking over the night stand.

"Hi Wayne! We got your bullet for you," said Roger from ballistics.

"Now wait! You got...say again...it can't be...now run that by me again. I thought you said you found a bullet. How could you find a bullet in those little thin steaks!?"

"No, it was lodged in the neck roast. I thought you knew that," said Roger.

"No, we included the neck just for good police work," I said. "You mean to tell me the deer was shot in the neck?"

"Right as rain," said Roger. "It couldn't have gone very far with a .22 caliber bullet through its spinal column."

"I'll be right up, Rog," I said. "I'll see you about noon."

The X-ray taken by the crime lab was a real eye opener. The bullet stood out as a black mass lodged between the vertebrae of the neck. I wondered how an animal so badly wounded could have traveled even the short distance from the clearing to the tree blind. In this instance my opinion meant very little. Greater minds than mine would have to analyze the evidence. The neck roast was signed out from the crime lab and taken to the Mid-county veterinary clinic for the opinion of a professional.

'Doc' as he was commonly known readily accepted the challenge to dissect the neck and determine the degree of trauma delivered by the .22 caliber slug. The roast was placed on the examination table and the careful cutting began. The path of the bullet was traced from its entrance on the right side of the neck to where it was retrieved in the middle of the spinal column. The damage to the spinal cord was assessed and Doc stated his opinion that the deer may have been able to travel after being so wounded, but not very far. He also indicated a willingness to testify in court. When you have an experienced, competent, smiling expert witness working with you, life is good.

The trial was the usual expected circus with all the motions, objections and "whereases", punctuated by the surprise of the bullet laden neck roast. Doc fielded all the mocking questions fired from the defense attorney with good humored expertise. When the defense attorney attempted to introduce doubt as to his credentials, Doc began answering the questions with fifty dollar words like 'intervertebral space', and 'striations', and 'intramuscular inclusions' and several other terms of doctor speak. The questions soon reverted back to 'just the facts'. When the State rested its case there was no doubt as to the outcome of the trial. The defense put on a nominal show and it was time to break for lunch, after which the jury would begin its deliberation.

The Ponderosa Steakhouse was my choice for the noon meal. I had promised Doc that I would buy lunch and somehow I just knew he'd order a T-bone steak.

The jury took a whole fifteen minutes to return a verdict of guilty. In the penalty phase the defense attorney objected to the mandatory sentence of five days in jail under the charge of 'willful illegal taking of deer'. The objection stated that the term 'willful' was not defined by law, nor was it determined that Oscar had 'willfully' killed the deer. Taking it under advisement, the judge agreed with the defense attorney and sentenced Oscar to a stiff fine and revoked his hunting privileges for four years, with no jail time. Because of this determination the State law was later changed to remove the term 'willful', making it a landmark case of sorts.

For a short time after this case some bitterness lingered between Oscar and Louie. The hard feelings between two neighbors did not last however and they were once again friends. Oscar was never again arrested for poaching and I believe he must have reformed. Either that or he began checking the area more carefully for tree blinds.

Rescues

It has been my experience that people, as a rule, do not like to be rescued. Perhaps it is the embarrassment of being in a situation that requires the attention of being rescued, or in some situations, the person being rescued having to admit that they put themselves in their predicament through negligence or folly. Even when in a 'life or death' state, aid is often refused. "I got this. Let me walk out of the woods by myself," was the statement made by a heart attack victim who had just been revived by paramedics. He was placed on a stretcher and suffered a second heart attack while being carried down the trail to the ambulance.

Drowning is most often a silent tragedy. The victim wildly waving his arms with head and shoulders above water loudly screaming "Help! Help!" is the material of comic books. A drowning victim is usually barely visible, weakly paddling, head only half out of the water, hoping against hope to somehow get out of the water without having to give in and cry for assistance. Once while swimming with my daughter in Higgins Lake I happened to see her slip beneath the waves and not immediately resurface. She was near a dock so I was not overly concerned as I located her and pulled her from the water. After coughing up a small amount of lake water Becky told me that she had become tired, couldn't breathe, and probably would have drowned had she not been helped. She was five years old. The occupation of a life guard is more difficult than most people think.

The career of a police officer offers opportunities to participate in many different types of rescues. House fires and automobile accidents are the most common for the Sheriff's deputy or State Trooper, while the conservation officer is selected to locate lost individuals, stranded or injured persons, and the victims of medical emergencies in the wild. Outdoor rescues are often 'handed off' to the conservation officer because they are more equipped for travel in harsh conditions or may have navigation and off road transportation capabilities not possessed by other police agencies.

One late October in 1987 the call went out for an officer to volunteer to assist the CO in Chippewa County. Bear season, waterfowl season and archery deer season had descended upon him simultaneously and he was simply overwhelmed. After the first week the hunters would thin out and activity would subside, but he really needed help for the first five days. I could not believe that I was the only volunteer.

CO Mike welcomed me into his spacious log home located on a bluff overlooking the St Marys River. A sweeping curve in this beautiful waterway offered a breathtaking view of great lakes freighters in their voyages up bound and down bound on the river. Mike had a telescope mounted on a tripod before his large picture window from where he could observe the vessels and chronicle their passing. His notebook recorded the passing of many foreign, ocean going ships as well. The autumn leaves mingled with bright evergreens below the bluff making for a breathtaking view. It was a shame to have to leave the appreciation of this scenery and put on the uniform.

Afternoon patrol was a pleasant affair. Bear baits were checked and one raft of decoys set in a shallow bay was noted, it being illegal to leave decoys out overnight in those waters. Late afternoon brought an overcast sky that transformed into gale force winds and heavy rain as we drove back to Mike's home.

At ten PM a call from the Michigan State Police interrupted our pleasant evening in the warm cabin. A group of three waterfowl hunters had not returned from hunting on the St. Mary's River, and it was feared that they were lost or stranded. The approximate location was given, and Mike and I saddled up, hitching the boat to the truck and survival suits donned.

The trip to the boat launch took longer than usual, the heavy rain obscuring visibility to nearly zero. Arriving at the launch site we were relieved to be blessed with a lull in the storm. Seas were still running at three to four feet in the river but would be subsiding soon with the dying of the wind.

Weather information had predicted this break, and the storm was to resume within the hour, accompanied by a shift in the wind from westerly to northeasterly. The boat ramp was of the type referred to as 'rustic', and runoff water made launching difficult as the pickup and boat trailer slid down the muddy apron of the ramp, stopping just in time at the water's edge. The patrol boat was set afloat, the truck parked and we embarked through the misty gloom for the last known location of our hunters.

The St Mary's River is a vast waterway. The main channel affords a good depth for the navigation of large ships and is maintained by the Army Corps of Engineers. Aside from this the many islands and bays on each side offer a sportsman's paradise. They also offer a hopeless maze for CO's searching for lost hunters after nightfall. We were lucky this night. At one point the river widens to nearly half a mile. In the middle of this wide area a sunken island rises to within three feet of the surface. Our hunters, caught by the storm, had capsized and washed to this shallow area. They were standing waist deep in the cold water. A very wet Yellow Labrador retriever sat, shivering on a floating, overturned duck hunting boat which appeared to be anchored nearby.

Upon pulling up to the hunters we had expected an eager, thankful greeting. To our surprise the hunters did not appear to be distressed about their situation in the least. The trio was made up of two adults and what appeared to be a boy in his late teens. All wore heavy, waterproof clothing and chest waders. The dog, perhaps the most realistic of the group, swam over and clambered aboard our boat.

"We're okay, we'll just wait until daylight'" said the tallest of the three. It was difficult to believe what we were hearing. Daylight was seven hours away with another storm due to hit at any minute. These folks just weren't aware of their plight. They may not have wanted to leave their boat. Often a snowmobiler, going through the ice on a lake, will keep a tight hold on the handlebars, riding the machine all the way to the bottom, perishing there. The attachment of a man to his toys is strong.

"Gentlemen you're going to have to come with us. You can pick up the boat tomorrow. When the next storm hits it's going to wash the three of you right out into the deep water," said Mike.

Reluctantly the three hunters joined the Retriever in our vessel and we departed for shore. The boat was trailered and the hunters were reunited with their vehicle and trailer at another launch site. Shortly thereafter the storm resumed with its predicted ferocity and Mike and I thankfully returned to his residence.

Two months later I received a letter from a large pizza corporation. A letter of thanks for our life saving endeavor on the St Mary's River was accompanied by coupons for four deluxe pizzas. Mike and I had rescued the CEO of the pizza company. Now he was most grateful, sending the coupons out of appreciation. I called Brian, the district supervisor.

Explaining the situation I asked "What should I do with these coupons? We're not allowed to accept gratuities."

Brian replied "I wouldn't say that those are gratuities as such. Do you think he's "bought" you in hopes of some future favor?"

"Of course not," I said. "He's just expressing his appreciation."

"Then if you really feel strongly about it, give them to your kids. I'm sure they'll share."

On the last day of the rifle deer season in late November of 1987 Sheri Van Poole and I were finishing our patrol in the North Fox forest. Snow had been falling heavily all afternoon and had turned the woods into a snow enshrined wonderland. The highway however, had been turned into a dangerous skating rink. Turning onto highway M-35 from North Fox road we encountered dangerous driving conditions that rapidly deteriorated as we traveled north on our way to Escanaba. At fuller Park we stopped to assist several cars that had slid off the road. The State Police were notified and the wrecker dispatched.

One particular skid mark caught my attention. It looked as if one vehicle had struck the Rapid River bridge and skidded down out of sight on the west side of the highway. Walking over the bank my flashlight caught sight of a small compact car, badly damaged in the front, at the bottom of the ditch.

The car was upright, sitting in a pool of gasoline. The fuel tank had evidently ruptured and fumes were strong in the air. One small spark could cause a violent explosion. Two occupants sat in the vehicle, staring forward as if in shock. Looking through the windshield I shouted to the passengers, a man appearing to be in his late seventies and a woman of equal age, "Do not turn your heads," fearing neck or back injuries.

Normal practice would have been to disconnect the battery. In this case I did not dare for fear of causing a spark which might ignite the gasoline fumes.

The passenger appeared to be unharmed and able to leave the car on her own. The driver would have to be removed by the paramedics, appearing to have back and neck injuries. The driver's door would have to be removed to rescue the driver on a back board. Returning to the patrol car I retrieved a ten millimeter wrench to remove the door while Sheri directed traffic.

Returning to the damaged car I noticed that the lady was still seated in the passenger's seat as I began removing the door.

"Ma'am," I said. "Any spark could cause this car to catch fire. You're going to want to get out. Now."

The lady said nothing, looking forward, a serene expression on her face.

"Ma'am, you need to get out. If this car explodes, you're going to die right with us," I said, trying to sound even more assertive.

"I know," she said almost in a whisper. Then I got it. Many years ago she had said "Wherever thou go-est, I shall go. To death do us part." This was a promise being kept. Man and wife, they had pulled in the same harness for probably sixty years, and she wasn't leaving now. Whatever happened to her mate was going to happen to her as well.

With tears misting my eyes and a lump in my throat I finished removing the door as the ambulance pulled up and removed the driver. Only then did his wife leave the car and allow me to help her up the slippery bank.

Another dark December day found me looking out on yet another snow storm. Temperatures had dropped to nearly zero and I was anticipating a nice, warm afternoon of watching television when that darned phone disrupted my plans. Mr. Gustafson who lived in Menominee had not heard from his brother, an old bachelor in his seventies, and was concerned for his well-being. I was familiar with Ole Gustafson, knew where he lived, and reassured Mr. Gustafson that I would check on his brother and call him back.

Ole Gustafson lived in an old farm house built before the days of insulation and high efficiency furnaces. Pulling into the Gustafson driveway I noted that no smoke emanated from the chimney. No answer at the door indicated that something might be amiss and took the liberty of opening the unlocked door and walking into the frigid farmhouse kitchen.

Creosote soot coated the high ceiling and down the walls to waist level. On the wood cook stove sat a ten quart pail full of solidly frozen ice. The fire had gone out in the wood stove and a quick trip up the roof ladder proved the chimney to be solidly plugged with creosote. My shout to Ole Gustafson was answered by a low moan from the bed room off the small living room.

Ole Gustafson lay in bed, fully clothed, boots sticking out from beneath a sparse quilt. To my questions as to his well-being Ole answered that he was fine; maybe a little cold, but otherwise doing just fine. His complexion had a waxy yellow pallor often worn by the no longer living. His ankles were ice cold and he did not respond when I pinched the skin. He bid me good day as if he believed that I would leave him in this condition.

Calling the rescue squad I moved the few pieces of furniture to expedite the paramedics when they removed Ole. My friend was going to make a trip to the emergency room, no matter who had to pay the bill.

The next day a member of the rescue squad called saying that Ole was resting peacefully. It had been necessary to remove half of one foot and several toes from the other, being frozen solid. Ole had been entering the final stages of hypothermia and would not have lasted many more hours.

All the people who were rescued were grateful once the adventure was over, even though they were reluctant to accept help at first. If a lesson is to be learned it would be "When in trouble, ask for and accept help." When called upon to help, ignore any refusals to accept help as long as you're confident that the rescue is necessary. We can all have a good laugh and live it down once the dust settles.

Repeat Customers

Throughout my career I have become increasingly convinced that there exist certain people whom we are destined to encounter repeatedly. Be it a phenomenon, natural law or whatever you want to label it, you're just going to see these persons over and over, though you may have absolutely nothing in common, and may live many miles apart. Normally an encounter with someone that would result in his or her arrest happens only once. Any more often than that and the poacher would be referred to as a 'frequent flier'. One such individual was Thomas Alvin Tucker (Don't call me Tommy!). Though he lived more than one hundred miles away our first of several encounters occurred within a half mile of the city of Stephenson, right in my own back yard, so to speak.

The rifle deer season of 1984 had been extremely busy. Large numbers of deer throughout the county worked in concert with liberalized bag limits to attract many hunters; residents and non-residents as well. In spite of an influx of conservation officers from other districts to assist, long hours of dealing with the public had caused our energy and patience to wear thin. During this deer season, forest fire supervisor Joe Noah worked as my partner. Joe's many years of experience and willingness to work any and all hours made him the ideal backup officer.

One night late in the season Joe and I were sitting at Granny's field, literally on the edge of town. Normally we would have worked out in the farmlands had it not been for several poaching complaints called in from the west Stephenson area. Darkness had fallen and we had just settled into a concealed driveway when an old, black Ford pickup came struggling past. A short distance south of our hiding spot the truck stopped and shined a hay field on the west side of the road.

Pulling out behind the pickup without using my headlights I crept up behind the vehicle, activating my headlights and blue strobes when we were fifty feet apart. Rather than pull over the driver hit the accelerator and burned rubber as he sped away. It was surprising how fast that old truck could go. Within a quarter mile we swung into a right hand ninety-degree curve, tires squalling from both vehicles as we barely negotiated the corner. By now I had activated the siren and the ear splitting noise further added to the confusion and stress of the pursuit.

As we straightened our course and headed west I suddenly heard the loud bellow of Joe's deep Italian baritone voice. "Hey, pull that #$%* truck off the #$%&* road! NOW!" Joe had opened the passenger door despite our speed of some eighty miles an hour and was standing on the rocker panel, holding onto the door top and roof gutter, shouting at the poachers. To my surprise the truck immediately pulled over and stopped.

Running up to the driver's side of the truck I saw the driver frantically trying to help the passenger unload the bolt action high powered rifle between them on the seat. Opening the door, I grasped him by both shoulders and 'assisted' him from the vehicle. It was like trying to pull a two hundred pound frightened cat from a tree. Once out of the truck the poacher continued to fight. Eventually it occurred to him that he was just digging himself a deeper hole and he surrendered. While waiting for his summons for hunting deer with the aid of an artificial light the driver, identified as Thomas Alvin Tucker asked, "Who is that guy who was hollering?"

"That's my partner, Joe," I said. "He helps me during deer season."

"Man I could hear him over the siren. Scared the crap out of me," Said Thomas.

"Well Tommy, here's your citation. You can handle it by mail. The court will send you a letter," I said.

"That's THOMAS, not Tommy!" he retorted.

"Are you related to the teacher here at the high school?" I asked.

"Yeah, that's my uncle. He's from the Garden Peninsula, too. Don't tell him I'm over here, okay?"

The next June we were working a group patrol on the Garden Peninsula. Illegal commercial gill netters had been heavily working the waters of Big Bay de Noc and it was time to work a sting operation to curtail the wanton poaching. Officer Earl from Rapid River and myself had been assigned to work back-up. This meant staying concealed at various positions on the peninsula while providing protection to several spotters who were placed at strategic points on the shoreline, waiting for the arrival of the illegal gill- netters. Once the illegal fishermen were observed lifting their nets, officers who had been waiting offshore in fast boats would be contacted and would swoop in, apprehending the poachers.

The afternoon went quietly with Earl and me sitting on the hood of the patrol car in an old abandoned gravel pit. The warm sun felt good, and if not for the blackout rule requiring absolute silence, we would have had several boxes of pistol ammunition on the patrol car hood, practicing on our favorite targets; the white plastic lids from the five gallon pails of the Ansell Corporation.

The crackling of gravel stones under tires brought us to high alert. It was Earl's district supervisor. "We've been made boys! Time for plan 'B'."

As usually happened, someone somewhere had slipped up and the bad guys were tipped off. As soon as we discovered that we'd been 'busted', officer Earl and I were to drive through the village of Garden to create a diversion while other officers picked up the spotters and we departed the area.

At a stop sign in Garden the patrol car's right side window was loudly 'smacked' by the fist of a passenger on a passing three wheeled ORV, nearly breaking the window. As the ORV sped south out of town Earl pursued, as much to occupy the fleeing bad guys as to perhaps apprehend them for operating an unlicensed vehicle on the highway. Two miles south of town the ORV made a right angle turn a hundred feet short of the corner and crashed into the ditch. Both occupants were unhurt, the passenger fleeing on foot; the driver preferring to stand and fight.

I must say that the driver put up a fantastic fight, but something about that two hundred pound wrestler seemed familiar.

"Tommy, is that you?" I asked.

"It's THOMAS, Dammit!" exploded Thomas. "Coleman? What are YOU doing over here?!"

It is said that enemies who somehow end up in the same fox hole during the melee of war, if allowed to talk for thirty seconds, cannot shoot one another; each recognizing the humanity in the other. Thus it seemed with 'Thomas' and me. We immediately ceased our fighting and walked up to the patrol car. Thomas accepted his ticket without argument, but before we were out of earshot he shouted "And it's THOMAS!"

Later that summer it was again time for a sting on the Garden. Following up on reports that numerous small, fast boats had been looting and pillaging the waters off the south end of the peninsula, undercover officers had rented a small summer cottage just north of Fairport, near a private boat launch.

Seven Conservation Officers were assigned to stake out in the cottage and keep the small harbor under surveillance. The plan was, that after observing several boats launch with illegal nets, the crew in the cottage would conceal themselves on the shore and jump the netters when they returned, confiscating their boat, fish and nets. The water pump in the cottage was not functioning, and the crew would be assigned to the house for as long as a week. This meant no showers or shaves for the duration of the stakeout. Guess who drew the short straw and got the cottage duty?

We deployed under the cover of darkness. To this day I do not know what the outside of the cottage looks like. Immediately after jumping from the van side door onto the front porch we set about quickly getting settled and grabbing a few hours of sleep.

The netters would be up and at 'em early.

Dawn found us glued to the windows facing the bay. Several boats pulled in at day break, but being unable to separate the guilty ones from the honest hook and liners, also known as 'sporties', we spent our time recording boat numbers and physical descriptions. The boat numbers would be telephoned in to ascertain the ownership of the vessels, and we could separate the sheep from the goats with that information.

The cottage water pump was indeed not functional. Being an old worn-out shallow well jet pump it would need special priming procedures to pull water from even a few feet underground. One of the R.A.P. officers who had arrived the day before had started the pump and left it run under the illusion that it might somehow suddenly start working. Of course this was the worst thing a person could do to an already partially worn out pump. Everyone had given up and resigned himself to a week-long hitch of smelling like the bottom of a bird cage.

After two days of surveillance, taking boat numbers and physical descriptions we were nearing the time when we would have to decide which group of illegal netters we would be arresting. Standing in the window, smelling myself and those around me, I could see that this just wasn't going to work. I had some experience with water pumps and knew that if the pump were severely worn, it might still be made to work, but more than likely not. Maybe I could just take a look at it and see...

The attached garage contained the water pump along with five gallons of clean water; our ration for the next few days. Knowing that I would never be forgiven for squandering our only source of water, I decided to take a gamble. Finding a pair of vise grip pliers I pinched closed the flexible line between the pump and the tank. Removing the top plug from the pump with an ancient adjustable wrench, I filled the pump with water from the sacred supply can. After several seconds the bubbling stopped, indicating that the pump body was solidly filled with water. If even a single bubble remained in the pump, the priming water would be lost and I would be in deep trouble with six very smelly CO's. After firmly screwing the top plug back into the pump I said a silent prayer and flipped the switch to the 'on' position.

The pump sprang to life, lugged down, and appeared to be sucking water. Slowly I released the grip of the pliers on the flexible line. The pressure instantly fell from forty pounds to zero and the pump began an empty sounding rattle. Dang it, lost the prime! Once more I closed off the flex line and filled the pump. By now I was committed. If I lost this next attempt, I might as well open the door and start running. If the CO's bullets didn't get me, the Garden boys would. Turning the switch back to 'on' I waited until the pump had built up as much pressure as it ever would; about forty-five pounds. This time I released the pressure on the flex line ever so slowly, almost imperceptibly. The pressure gauge dropped to twenty pounds, then to ten. Suddenly, the pump motor lugged down and the gauge shot back up to forty-five pounds; a sign that the connection between the pump and the underground supply was complete. Showers all around. Me first! There would not be enough pressure to shut the pump off, but no one was complaining.

Finally the R.A.P. officers decided that tonight was the night. Three illegal gill net boats had launched that afternoon and the time would never be better to make a bust on whichever boat came in first. Surveillance had shown the boats to be launching during the afternoon and returning after two AM.

Under the cover of darkness our group of five CO's made our way down to the shore. The two R.A.P. officers remained at the cottage to keep up the appearance of two beach bums enjoying a summer off from college, and to maintain communications.

We set up under the spreading boughs of a large Cedar tree, with branches touching the ground. The lack of deer, thanks to the poaching of the locals, allowed cedars in the area to grow low; giving cover to birds, small woodland creatures, and of course CO's. The small harbor was a mere hundred feet away, allowing for a fast pounce on any bad guy's boat coming into the harbor. Lying on the fist sized rocks under the tree we attempted to maintain absolute silence. We were cognizant of the fact that at any time, we could be visited by someone walking down to the harbor, to give a shore location signal to a returning boat. Even though it was mid-June the rocks upon which we reposed were cold, as was the mist that continued to settle during the night. Our shivering was beyond our control. We would just have to hope that anyone coming down to the harbor would be making enough noise of their own that they wouldn't detect the chattering of several sets of teeth.

At two AM a vehicle pulled into the harbor, its headlights sweeping across our location, nearly giving away our presence.

The lights extinguished and two locals walked down to the harbor, waiting for a returning boat. For a half hour or so we listened to them conversing about illegal netting, and the locations of each other's nets. Finally the pair gave up their wait and departed. One of them actually threw a lit cigarette butt into our Cedar tree.

At three AM an individual later identified as a sixteen-year-old brother to one of the illegal fishermen walked down to the harbor. Presently the distant sound of an outboard motor could be heard approaching. The youngster began waving a 'glow stick', a fluorescent tube made to glow for several hours and serve as a night time signal.

Upon the arrival of the gill netters at the small harbor, the youngster secured the open twenty-one foot fiberglass boat to the dock and the three-man crew began unloading a number of boxes of whitefish.

Trying our best to maintain silence, our six-man troupe slowly stood, stretched, and ran down to the harbor, surrounding the group before they could discover our presence. Upon our sergeant's greeting of "Conservation officers! Hold it right there!" all three jumped into the harbor and began swimming out into the bay. Several CO's untied the boat and followed two of the swimmers. Seeing that the third member of the party was swimming towards shore, off to the south side around the harbor entrance, I ran across a small spit of land to intercept him as he came ashore.

My swimmer reached land before I could make contact and ran towards the woods, but it was obvious that much of his energy had been sapped by the cold bay water. As I caught him I could see that he was stumbling and my tackle completed his trip to the ground. He began to thrash from side to side, trying to break my full nelson grip. Something once again seemed very familiar about this big fellow.

"Tommy, is that you?" I asked.

"Dammit, it's THOMAS! Coleman? Man ain't there any

other CO's in the state?" Thomas once again ceased his fighting and we walked back to the harbor.

Both poacher and CO alike were surprised to see us walking back, talking and joking as if we were long lost cousins. With so many arrestable people in both Delta and Menominee County as well as the number of CO's available to do the arresting, I could not for the life of me figure out why Thomas and I kept crossing paths. Cuffs were applied and the guilty trio was placed in the van for transport to the Delta County Jail. Two CO's and myself transported the stripped down, high-powered boat back to Escanaba across Big and little Bays de Noc. At sixty-miles an hour.

I was not surprised later that fall when VCO Nate related that he had met a young man while gassing up his car in Manistique. Conversing while filling their vehicles, the young man spoke of living on the Garden peninsula and that he used to make his living by gill netting and dodging the DNR.

"Did he give his name?" I asked.

"Yeah, same as the teacher. Tommy Tucker."

Nate jumped back in surprise when I shouted in his face "That's THOMAS, you dolt!"

Pilgrims

"Two one-thirty-one from eighty-nine."

"Station eighty-nine, go ahead."

"We have a lost hunter in the Westman Dam area. Six hunters are here at the post. They were supposed to meet at the parking lot north of the dam, and one hunter didn't show at sunset."

Big Ben was working the desk at the State Police post. I could always count on him for an entertaining complaint. Fortunately I was near the highway G-12/Westman Dam road intersection, only two miles from the dam.

"Station 89 I am on G-12 at this time near Westman road. I will be enroute your station within the hour. I'll check the parking lot to see if our hunter has arrived and come in to interview the complainants," I said.

Darkness had settled only half an hour earlier and my suspicion was that the 'lost' hunter would appear unscathed within a short period of time. As I crossed the Westman dam, almost as if on cue, a bright orange clad figure strode into view, waving to me as I approached.

Rolling the patrol car window down I asked "Are you one of a hunting party of seven?"

"Well, I was, but they seem to have abandoned me!" Exclaimed the tall, gray haired hunter. He appeared to be in his sixties, but fit and trim.

"I think I can re-unite you with your comrades," I said. "Let's unload your rifle and I'll give you a lift."

"I can't figure out why they left me," said our hunter as we motored south on Westman road.

"I think they were just really concerned about you," I said.

"Well, they could have waited longer. I wasn't going to come out before dark," he said.

The group of six hunters were as joyous as puppies to see their comrade once they were brought together at the Post. Profuse appreciation was expressed to Big Ben and I, and the happy group departed.

Once we were alone Big Ben leaned back in his office chair, crossed his arms and gazed off to the side as if searching some horizon many miles in the distance. Anytime I witnessed this type of body language from Ben I knew that I was about to be subjected to one of his philosophical points. "Ya know what I think?" Without waiting for an answer he continued, "I think that once it got dark, all the 'Pilgrims' piled into the car and raced here in a big panic and left the 'Hunter' in the woods. Dorks!"

Wow! Big Ben often referred to the occasional good citizen as 'dumb' or an 'idiot', but this particular invective was reserved for only the most extreme example of ineptitude. You had to be a special kind of 'stupid' to merit the description of 'Dork' from Big Ben. His reference to 'Pilgrims' also signified a higher level of incompetence in Ben's book of personal evaluations. To Ben a 'Pilgrim' was an over eager, naive individual, always impatient to jump in without planning or knowledge of the consequences. This could describe rescuer and victim alike; sometimes both at the same time. A Pilgrim might be the hiker on the mountain who sallies forth without proper outdoor gear, getting himself trapped and in need of rescue. On the other hand it might be that neighborhood watch member who shows up at an accident scene with all sorts of flashing lights on his car, just frothing at the mouth to be of assistance. "Give *them* the flare and let *them* direct traffic," Ben would say. "Let *them* get the burns on their nylon jacket."

Whether or not one agrees with Ben in his definition of 'Dorks' or 'Pilgrims', there does seem to be a faction of society that simply cannot help themselves when it comes to getting in the way of progress. One prime example is the case of the lost hunter.

One late November evening I was called to a farm on a side road three miles east of the village of Daggett. Gerald Thayer had not returned home from deer hunting after sundown and the family, out of concern for his well-being, had called several neighbors. Soon a group of worried citizens had gathered at the Thayer residence and a loosely structured search party was organized, more than eager to take to the darkened forest in search of Gerald. Mrs. Thayer called the State Police to advise that the search party would be scouring the woods in search of her husband. Recognizing the potential for even bigger problems the State Police notified me by radio and I rushed to the scene.

Arriving at the Thayer home I interviewed Mrs. Thayer who, although extremely worried, did affirm that Gerald had been warmly dressed and was in reasonably good physical condition. My assurance that Gerald would more than likely be making an appearance momentarily did little to assuage her fears. Stepping onto the deck at the front door of the Thayer house I addressed the group of anxious neighbors armed with flashlights, ready to adjourn to the wilderness in search of the missing Mr. Thayer. Looking out at the small crowd I was reminded of the Sheriff in those B grade movies, addressing a lynch mob.

"Listen up!" I said. "Mr. Thayer is more than likely not lost. He is familiar with the area and in good physical condition. If he somehow got turned around he'll just listen for traffic and walk out to a nearby road. If we go into the woods we'll just end up with more lost people." The urge to use the term 'Pilgrims' instead of 'people' was strong, but I refrained.

"Yeah, but what will you say when we find him in the morning – dead!" shouted someone in the crowd.

"Calm down," I said, trying to sound reassuring. "Let's give it half an hour, and if he doesn't show we'll get the tracking dog. Without snow we have no idea where he's gone or where he may be."

The small crowd seemed to assent, breaking into small groups, mumbling amongst themselves. At that moment an old rusty pickup rattled into the yard. Happy cheers greeted Gerald as he stepped from the passenger's door of the truck. Mrs. Thayer ran to embrace Gerald. "Where have you been? We've been worried sick!" she exclaimed.

"Heck, I came out on the other side of the section," said Gerald. "I was having coffee with Einar Pelke. What's all the excitement about?" Most cases of reported lost hunters resulted in this type of happy ending in Menominee County.

Another mid-December night found me answering a call to a residence east of Wallace. One of the local residents, Ernie Truman had gone hunting in the Hayward Lake swamp and had not returned. The late hour of ten PM did raise some concern and I agreed to cruise the back roads around the lake in an effort to find his vehicle and his whereabouts.

At approximately eleven PM I pulled into the Hayward Lake boat launch and discovered Ernie's pickup sitting in the small parking lot, hooked to a boat trailer. A survey of the launch revealed the probable cause of Ernie's failure to return home. A half inch of crystal clear ice covered the channel leading out to the lake! Ernie had more than likely gone hunting on one of the two islands in the middle of Hayward Lake and become 'iced in'. One would think that while hunting on an island, small enough that one could see the lake at any given time, one might notice that with the drop in temperature, the lake would be freezing over. This hunter however, seemed to have become so enraptured with the beauty of his surroundings that he failed to notice the fact that the lake no longer sported ripples, or that a heavy chill was rapidly settling over the area. It takes a significant drop in the mercury to develop a skim of ice, but that's exactly what had happened.

Turning on the patrol car's public address system I spoke into the mike. "Ernie, this is Wayne Coleman. If you're on the north island, fire your gun once into the air." Absolute silence. I spoke again into the mike, "Ernie, if you're on the south island, fire once into the air." One explosion signaled Ernie's location. I then gave Ernie some instructions. "Ernie, do not, I repeat do not attempt to take your boat out onto the lake. Build a fire if you can so you can be located. We will have a rescue boat come out soon. If you understand, shout as loud as you can." Within moments a high pitched wail of "Okaaaaay!" could be heard. I radioed the Menominee county sheriff's department requesting the marine safety unit with their rescue boat.

As I waited for the Sheriff's unit Ernie's father-in-law, accompanied by several cars with a menagerie of boats in varying states of flotation ability pulled into the launch. Evidently someone had a police radio receiver and felt it their responsibility to organize a vigilante rescue posse. Jumping from their vehicles several of the local gentry ran to the water's edge shouting "Don't worry Ernie! We'll get ya!", and words to that effect. Considerable effort was required to quell the small mob, explaining to them that professional help was on the way. Their cheering would encourage Ernie to take to the water before rescue was at hand, creating even bigger problems should he capsize or fall into the lake. The good neighbors were not about to be thwarted, determined to launch their own boats in a rescue attempt.

"If one of your boats backs up to the launch, you're all going to be arrested for failing to obey the legal command of an officer," I threatened. Of course I couldn't prevent a citizen from launching his boat, but the ruse worked and the group chose to wait on shore for the marine unit.

The marine safety officers arrived within a half hour. Dressed in dry suits, they began the rescue procedure. Ice was broken as the flat bottomed John boat was launched and as the boat motored out to the lake both officers moved from front to back, causing the rocking of the craft to break the ice as they proceeded.

Within an hour the rescue unit had returned with a very cold but grateful Ernie and his small aluminum boat. After a nice hot shower and some supper Ernie would be joining the jolly folks of the vigilante group at the Wallace pub to retell the events of the day. I myself was happy that things had shaken out in a positive manner and continued on patrol.

A week later Sergeant Ben was working desk at the post when I stopped to fuel the patrol car. Having heard of the Hayward Lake adventure he asked me about the incident. I was happy to spend a half hour filling Ben in on the details.

"Good job," said Ben. "It's not easy to conduct a rescue operation by yourself. But when you have Pilgrims on both sides, now that's even worse. Bunch of Dorks!"

The Last Few Miles

W hen it comes to sport fishing, the Menominee River is actually two rivers in one. Nearly the entire length of the stream supports populations of fish that are confined to the river. Most of the river offers a fishery of Walleye, Northern Pike and pan fish. In the White Rapids reservoir, fisheries division has conducted an experiment that presents Tiger Muskellunge to anglers so inclined, and the northern waters and tributaries harbor populations of various species of trout. Sturgeon inhabit deep holes and power dam tail races along the way, and Catfish scrounge a living wherever they can.

From its inception far to the north, the Menominee River suffers the restrictions of its banks bordering Wisconsin and Michigan, traveling through forests, farm country, cities, towns, burgs and hamlets until it finally flows free into the waters of Green Bay between the twin cities of Menominee, Michigan and Marinette, Wisconsin. This waterway is in a constant state of evolution. It has served as a vehicle for the transportation of millions of board feet of Pine logs. It has absorbed uncountable tailings from iron and copper mines. It has suffered the indignity of countless tons of waste material from dairy barn yards and the runoff of fertilizer from farm fields. It has served as a handy end point for many septic fields. It was even host to a house of ill repute on a small island immediately downstream from the Koss Bridge during the logging era. Yet the river flows on, adapting and changing to meet each new challenge. The fishery continues to thrive, and sportsmen continue to enjoy nature's bounty.

The last few miles are unlike the first winding length of the watershed. At Hattie Street near the north side of Menominee, the Scott Paper dam serves as a barrier of access to Green Bay and the Great Lakes. Anadromous fish, those fish that journey upstream to spawn, are curtailed in their efforts to travel further, and are thus concentrated in a pool downstream from the dam, subject to the presentations of numerous lures offered by sports fishermen, hoping to catch that trophy of a lifetime.

Upon my assignment to Menominee County I was introduced to the Hattie Street fishery in a most abrupt manner. Smelt season was upon us, and patrol consisted of checking fishing licenses of smelt netters from numerous different states. Many smelt netters were of the belief that a fishing license was not required to catch a fish so small, and many an argument was endured as we attempted to explain that 'the user pays', no matter how small the fish. Summonses were issued and bonds were taken as we attempted to recover some respect for the resource. Ensuing years would see a diminishing of the smelt population as far as the river run fish were concerned, and our patrol efforts would concentrate on different species, such as Pike and Salmon.

As the lower river fishery continued to evolve, we as enforcers of the fish and game laws found it necessary to adapt our methods of patrol. It was no longer sufficient to appear on the scene and check licenses. With the advent of Salmon and Brown Trout, most of the fishermen were in possession of licenses. It was their methods of fishing that came into question.

"Snagging" is a method of fishing wherein a large treble hook is used, weighted with as much as several ounces of lead. The hook was cast into the stream, and the fisherman would jerk the line in an attempt to hook a fish as the illegal device was pulled rapidly through the water. Fish do not voluntarily bite on the hook, but are hooked in the body and hauled ashore by stout line and a heavy pole. In Michigan, Snagging is illegal. In Wisconsin, snagging is allowed in certain streams. Therein lay the problem. Was it legal to snag in the Menominee River, or was it not? The rule book was quite explicit. Snagging in the Menominee River was illegal on both sides. However, as could be expected, there were those who attempted to rely on the ambiguity of the confusing laws to escape the consequences if caught.

The problem was compounded by the lack of access to the Scott Paper dam. Our ability to patrol this area was limited to approaching the fishing area from Hattie Street. A hundred yards of open area gave away our presence as we walked to the access wall. Snaggers were able to cut their lines and dispose of their illegal hooks before we could make contact. It was obvious that, if allowed to continue, the fishery would suffer great losses as the Salmon, Trout, Walleye and Sturgeon were depleted by poachers who operated with impunity while we watched helplessly from a distance.

A visit to the Scott Paper Company offices in Marinette, Wisconsin took care of the problem in short order. The paper company had been suffering serious losses due to vandalism at the Hattie Street dam and warehouse from inconsiderate users of the site who had no compunction with littering, or throwing the occasional rock through the warehouse windows should they feel the urge. They had suffered enough, and were eager to accept our help. Keys to the warehouse were issued, and we began a number of stakeouts in an effort to curtail illegal fishing, as well as vandalism to the Scott Paper property. This opened a whole new vista of law enforcement, as well as many new experiences for this novice Game Warden.

Stakeout patrol in the Scott Paper dam warehouse was a definite boon to the resource, to say the least. One-way film was installed at strategic places on the warehouse windows, and fishermen were watched in relative safety from being detected. Numerous illegal activities were observed and a number of arrests were made that could not have been made by other means. Snaggers, fishermen without licenses, and over limits of fish were detected and arrests made. Litterbugs and vandals were caught and word soon circulated that the Scott Paper dam was not a good place to break the law.

In meeting the operators of the dam, I was made aware of a number of trespassing violations that had been taking place for several years. Fishermen had been anchoring at the face of the dam and climbing about the structure of the dam itself. City police officers had advised that there was virtually nothing they could do unless the operators were willing to personally file a trespassing complaint, which they were reluctant to do. I merely wrote the offenders tickets for trespassing, inviting them to meet me in court, which they, of course opted not to do, paying their fines instead. The remaining challenge was from the snaggers, who used any and all methods of evasion to escape arrest. Over time I became a court recognized expert at determining whether or not a fish had been foul hooked in the body, or had bit voluntarily by the presence or absence of hook marks in the mouth. I was able to convince the court that a fish hooked grievously in the body could not have gone on to legally bite on a lure presented by a legal fisherman.

Throughout this period of time many incidents and experiences happened that I shall never forget. Some of these involved 'The juvenile offender.'

For some reason, DNR law enforcement seemed to think that there was virtually nothing that could be done about the juvenile offender. It was true that juvenile court was able to do very little to punish the juvenile law breaker as far as criminal law was concerned, but somehow it seemed to have escaped everyone's attention that *civil* penalties could be assessed to persons of any age. Sport fish illegally taken could be assessed at ten dollars per pound, and all juveniles found in possession of illegally taken fish were thus charged. In the Menominee County Probate court they would be assigned to write an essay as to why their violation was detrimental to the resource, and charged ten dollars for each pound of illegal fish possessed.

Stakeout patrol in the warehouse was both fun and educational. In some ways it destroyed my feeling that most people were basically honest, and in other ways it restored my faith in humankind. Some fishermen would cheat at every opportunity, while others might release a trophy fish that had not been hooked directly in the mouth.

One day I witnessed the snagging of a number of Northern Pike by several juvenile fishermen. They would take their ill-gotten fish around the east end of the warehouse, out of sight. Several minutes later they would return without the fish. Sneaking out of the warehouse and conducting a search of the area, I was unable to find any sign of the illegally taken fish. I found this situation somewhat baffling.

At this point I should point out that, as far as the news media is concerned, police officers and doctors are easily baffled. Just pick up any newspaper, and the headlines will greet you with a statement such as "Crown jewels stolen! Police are baffled, but arrests are imminent." Don't worry folks, the cops are perplexed and puzzled, but we'll get the bad guys, don't you worry. To an extent it's true. We as officers of the law are often puzzled at circumstances we may encounter; but not for long. How the news media knows this, baffles me.

What really concerns me is the fact that doctors are equally susceptible to this phenomenon of bafflement. Often a terminally ill patient is found to have outlived all the months of projected survival given by members of the medical community. The patient is seen on television, proclaiming loudly that his doctors are 'totally baffled', saying to him: "You're supposed to be dead! Why are you still alive?" I am happy that our patient has survived in spite of the negative opinions of the physicians. What worries me is that when I enter the hospital for my next back surgery, I will encounter hordes of medical practitioners, wandering around with big question marks over their heads. How does one submit to anesthesia and the knife under these conditions? But I digress.

It was discovered that our juvenile pike snaggers were selling the fish to a buyer who had pulled up in a car, paying a dollar per fish and fleeing across the Hattie Street Bridge into Wisconsin. A little fast footwork resulted in several arrests and the curtailment of this problem.

One person I shall never forget was a fisherman I will refer to simply as "Robin Hood", because of his propensity to give away his illegally taken fish to those who could use the food. I first met him as a juvenile, when he would snag fish at the wall up near the face of the dam. Being a person of no visible means to pay the restitution, he simply let the costs build up until his seventeenth birthday when he became a 'keeper'. Once a person has attained the age of seventeen he is considered an adult, responsible for his actions and able to be arrested and incarcerated under the law.

Upon our first encounter, he gave his address as 'seventeen-seventeen, Seventeenth Street'. Yeah, sure, and my name is Howdy Doody. As it turned out this was his actual address, and his mother was distraught at my bringing him home to be released into her custody.

As the years went by we developed a sort of Pat Garrett/

Billy the Kid relationship. He knew I was the Game Warden, and I knew he was the poacher. And we were good with that. The district judge, however, literally tore his hair out, trying to come up with some way to make Robin obey the law. He put him in jail. He assessed huge fines. He revoked his fishing license. He ordered him to buy a fishing license. Nothing seemed to work. The final excuse was always "Your honor, I just can't help myself. I can't stop fishing!"

I swear, that boy could catch fish in a bowl of chicken soup. One rainy, cold day I spent the afternoon in the Scott Paper warehouse watching the few fishermen hardy enough to brave the wind and rain to fish at the dam. This was during one of the periods that Robin was forbidden by the court to fish. I watched as Robin cautiously strode down the grass walkway to the wall near the face of the dam. No fish of any kind had been caught this stormy November week, and fishing was more an exercise in futility than anything else.

Looking suspiciously about, Robin pulled a coil of mono-filament fishing line from his pocket, wound up and pitched a weighted jig head and twister lure into the current. Almost immediately he hooked an eighteen inch Brown Trout. I was immediately behind him as he pulled the fish ashore. After several minutes of small talk I asked "Well, what do you want this time, Robin? Fish contrary to the decree of the court, or possession of trout without a license?"

"Let's go with the 'no license' thing. I can just pay that without having to face the judge," said Robin.

It got to where I would be driving down the street in Menominee and see Robin walking on the sidewalk. Knowing that a warrant was out for his arrest, I would simply pull over to the curb, and Robin would get in, knowing that he would never outrun me. I would always implore Robin to get his life in order; to stop breaking the law, and he began to say that he would have to get things straightened out if he was to lead a responsible adult life. I hope it finally worked out for him.

Another time found me observing what one fisherman thought was the Sturgeon of a lifetime. His rod was bent nearly double and his line ran upstream and downstream, into the tailrace and back up the rip current. After more than an hour he was able to beach his catch. It turned out to be a piece of sheet metal, approximately a foot square, hooked by a small hole in its center. The scrap of steel rode the currents like a kite, creating a very fishlike action, giving the angler a thrill he would never forget. He did take the piece of steel with him upon leaving the site. Maybe it's on his living room wall where a trophy fish would have been.

One sunny May afternoon I was killing a few hours in the warehouse. Fishing was slow and the spring runs were almost finished, save for a few Sturgeon that were cruising along close to the bank as they sought the ideal location to lay their eggs. As I watched, two fishermen walked down to the bank and began searching the water. No two fellows could have been more unevenly matched. One was tall and extremely thin. His companion was short and corpulent. "Mutt and Jeff" would have described them perfectly. Mutt was the first to spot a large female Sturgeon. Throwing out his spoon, he purposely snagged the fish as the lure was pulled over its back. The fight was on, and Mutt played the fish as it struggled through the current, trying to shake the lure.

As the fish passed by again Jeff cast his lure and snagged the Sturgeon as well. Both anglers began to pull the suffering fish ashore. At that moment another person walked down the path to the fishing site. To me he was no more than just a passer-by, but Jeff turned and with an anguished look on his face, said something to Mutt. Mutt immediately pulled out a jackknife and cut his line. Jeff swiftly followed suit. Both fishermen reeled in their lines and ran; no, *sprinted* away and across the Hattie Street Bridge into Wisconsin.

Once again I was momentarily baffled. Leaving the building I confronted the fellow who had walked down to Mutt and

Jeff. His baseball cap advertised a local machine shop; Coleman machine. The name Coleman was emblazoned across the front of his cap in bright orange letters. That one name alone had caused the poachers to abandon their crime and flee in mindless terror. For a moment I felt like Puff, the Magic Dragon, the mere mention of whom would cause pirate ships to lower their flags. Then I remembered that I had just lost a good Sturgeon arrest. Dang! Snookered again! Oh well, at least I was no longer baffled.

Years have passed and a new company has assumed ownership of the power dam and warehouse. I think of the old place often and hope that the fishing resource is still being protected with the diligence it deserves. I hope that, for the last few miles of the Menominee River, the beat goes on.

One Lucky Lady

It was Friday, the end of the first week of the rifle deer season. Hunting conditions had been ideal and many deer had already been taken. Temperatures in the twenties and an inch of fresh snow had kept the deer moving and easy to track.

The Wildlife station at the Stephenson field office had checked a record number of animals this week. They had been busy trying to shorten the long line of successful hunters since daybreak. While enjoying that first cup of coffee of the day, I visited with the orange clad Nimrods as biologists recorded data from their trophies; presenting them with their Successful Hunter patch for their co-operation. The bottom of the cup of Joe was my signal to get out on patrol. Hopefully today could be spent visiting hunting camps, checking the success of hunters, soon to begin their journey home. This would be the day to verify that deer were legally tagged, and that bag limits were not exceeded.

Snakey Lake road was covered with a dusting of snow from the previous night. The absence of tracks served to indicate that Most of the hunters were at camp and could be contacted as they returned from their blinds for coffee at mid-morning. For the moment I was captivated by the snow on the Tamarack boughs, twinkling in the sun with a million reflected rainbow gems. Just as I began to enjoy the slow cruise through this sunny, morning winter wonderland, the radio crackled to life.

"Two one thirty-one from eight nine," said Sergeant Gary.

"Eight nine, go ahead."

"We have a complaint out east of Dog town. Hunter shot a dwelling," said Gary. "Stop at the Robin Harrington residence."

"We're clear eight nine. Estimated time of arrival will be twenty minutes," I replied. "I'll be coming from the Oxbow area."

"Eight nine is clear."

Robin Harrington was visibly agitated and met me at the end of his driveway. "I'm about to go next door and clean house. They've got way too many hunters over there, and they're shooting all over the place! Now they've almost killed my daughter!" he shouted.

"Okay, I know it's hard to do, but please try to calm down. I need to see just what happened, and I have to collect accurate facts," I said to Mr. Harrington who was red faced and in tears; having trouble standing still.

"Come on in the house and I'll show you what happened," said Robin as he opened the kitchen door to the residence.

Maria Harrington, while somewhat shaken, calmly described the events of the previous several hours. The high school senior had been a cross country runner for the Stephenson team and I had been her coach since she joined the team as a freshman.

Her upstairs bedroom was the scene of the hunting accident.

"I was sitting on the bed, brushing my hair when something hit the outside of the house with a loud 'bang', and something that sounded like a giant bee came buzzing right past my head," Maria explained. "It hit up there on the steel part of the closet door and it's still stuck there."

The bullet had struck the second story bedroom wall on the north side of the house, just to the left side of a single window. It had passed through a layer of tough, Masonite siding, one inch of board sheeting, a coat of lath and plaster, and lodged in the upper track of the bedroom closet. Remarkably the bullet was intact, complete with its metal jacket. This would serve well in identifying the owner of the firearm, should the opportunity be presented.

To the north of the house a wide open field had been planted to winter wheat. No deer blinds were in evidence, although a hill prevented any detailed view of the property. The field was owned by Blaine Borkovich, a dairy farmer on the county road a half mile north of the Harrington home.

The bullet was retrieved as evidence, photographs were taken, and the Harrington family was assured that an investigation would be conducted. Robin Harrington was not convinced of the prospects of any success.

"They have people from all over hunting on that farm. They have no idea what kind of people are blazing away at everything that moves," insisted Robin. "I just want to go over there and give them a piece of my mind."

"Well, please trust me on this one," I said. "If I can find out who fired the careless shot, you can bet that he will be brought to justice."

It was sheer luck that the hunters at the Borkovich farm were all coming in for lunch as I pulled into the driveway. In all seven hunters had been hunting the eighty acre plot of land. While it did not appear to be a crowded situation, the fact that only thirty acres of the property were wooded changed the game considerably. It did indeed seem like a lot of hunters per forested acre. They stood around the patrol car in a circle as I explained the situation. "What we have here is a nearly fatal hunting accident. The house to the south was struck by a bullet a few hours ago, and I'm trying to find the hunter who took the shot. I'm sure it was an accident, but we need to clear this up."

One of the group stepped forward. "It couldn't have been us. We were driving that cedar swamp over to the west. We got some shooting in, but nobody shot any houses."

The deer drive. To my way of thinking it was one of the most unsafe methods of hunting ever used. Usually near the end of a hunting trip, hunters would often try to fill their remaining tags by chasing deer from the wooded cover in which they hid. Hunters would line up on one side of a wooded plot, spaced some fifty yards or so apart, while several other hunters would begin on the other side, moving slowly through the woods, herding the deer before them toward the posted hunters. The practice is unsafe because most of the shots are taken at running deer, either by the posted hunters shooting toward the drivers, or at each other as the deer run between them. Drivers also shoot toward the posted hunters if they see deer moving in their path. During my tenure in Menominee County one hunter was killed during a deer drive, and several others injured.

"Here's what I would like to do. Let me take your rifles for an hour or so. I'll give you a receipt, and you'll have them back for the afternoon's hunt. I'll run the ballistics on the guns and we'll eliminate them as suspect firearms." I had expected some resistance to this suggestion, and I was not disappointed.

"What if we refuse," said one of the group. "What then?"

"Well, the fact that the house was struck from the north by the bullet from a high powered rifle, and you're all hunting to the north with high powered rifles gives me probable cause to get a search warrant," I said. "The State Police would come out and make sure that nobody leaves while I go to Menominee and spend several hours getting the warrant, and I'd take the guns then. By the time things are finalized it will be long past sundown, and none of us will be happy. I'd really like to clear this up so we can all get back to what we really want to do."

Another of the group prevailed with common sense. "I say we give the officer the guns and get ourselves cleared so we can get back to hunting," he said. "I've only got this afternoon left to hunt before I have to go back home."

Guns were placed in their protective cases and receipts issued. The group was comprised of hunters from down state, Illinois and Indiana. Serial numbers were recorded along with contact information for each hunter. It was time to get into the science of this investigation.

In my back yard I had buried an old water heater tank with the top removed, standing on end. When filled with water and a screen basket placed at the bottom it served very well as a bullet catching device. A square of carpeting would be placed on top to prevent excessive splashing and the suspect firearm would be discharged into the tank. The screen basket would then catch the bullet. The projectile would be saved, along with the spent brass casing, for inspection by the ballistics division at the State Police crime lab. Over the years I'd had the opportunity to use this tank to catch a wide variety of bullets, from the seventeen caliber varmint rifle to an elephant gun. The only bullet to ever travel the full length of the four foot column of water and penetrate the screen basket...the twenty two rim fire.

This afternoon all seven deer rifles were taken to my residence and discharged into the tank. The bullets and spent casings were saved and cataloged for comparison with the bullet retrieved from the Harrington home.

Ballistics is a very exact science. Unique marks and scratches on the inside of each gun barrel leave marks on bullets that will be different from all other weapons. Matching one bullet with another is done under the high powered magnification of a microscope. If one of the deer rifles taken as evidence was the one that had shot through Maria's bedroom, we would soon know for certain. Likewise the brass casing expands when a bullet is fired. Unique scratches are made on each casing by the chamber as it is extracted from the gun. These scratches, along with machine marks made by the extractor serve as further identification, should spent casings be found at a crime scene.

All rifles were returned to their owners by 2:30 PM, well before 'Deer O'clock'. Now it was time to make the trip to the crime lab in Negaunee with the throttle to the front wall. If I hurried I could make it and log the evidence in before they closed for the week end.

Roger, the ballistics expert, looked the bullets over and was able to narrow the suspect slugs down to just three by the number of rifling grooves present on the copper jackets, and the diameter of each bullet. The bullet that had been taken from the Harrington house was a thirty caliber with four grooves, and three of the bullets to be tested fit this description. We would have the results some time during the next week, after microscopic comparison was made.

Something continued to bother me. How did the bullet find its way to the Harrington house? The hill should have blocked the path of any bullet fired in that direction. Perhaps the bullet had been a fluke, coming from some other location. Any other logical hunting land from where such a shot could have been fired was more than a mile away. While a high powered rifle can easily shoot the distance, the odds were just too great. I had to do more research.

Saturday morning dawned bright and sunny, making for perfect conditions to check out hunting locations on the Borkovich property. The afternoon sun of the previous day had melted the skiff of snow, making for difficult tracking, but revealing any evidence that may have fallen and disappeared in the snow. The north/south fence line of the wood lot to the west bordered the open field adjacent to the Harrington property. Walking along this line I could see the occasional small circle of packed grass indicating the places occupied by the four posting hunters from the previous day's deer drive. At the base of one large maple tree lay the shiny spent casing of a 308 caliber rifle. Someone had done some shooting, but in which direction?

Looking up into the branches of the maple I could see a small platform approximately fifteen feet off the ground. After climbing up onto the platform and taking a look around, I had my answers. From the elevated stand, the Harrington house was in plain view. A deer running across the crest of the hill could have easily come into a direct line with the second story of the home. A spent casing from the rifle would have fallen down through the branches, coming to rest on the west side of the tree. Right where I found it.

While on patrol the next Tuesday afternoon I was contacted by station eight nine, requesting that I call the crime lab. The results from ballistics were in.

"I've got your bullet," said Roger. "A dead-bang one hundred per cent positive identification. It's a 308 caliber belonging to Peter Hoyt from Alma. Come on up and get the slugs any time."

"Thank you much," I said. "I now have a spent casing that I may need to bring up, as well."

"We'll be happy to look at it for you."

As could be expected, Mr. Hoyt denied everything when I called and advised that he would be cited for the hunting accident. "No way! It just couldn't have happened. None of our bullets could have ever made it over that hill"

"Well, the bullet is a positive match from one fired from your gun," I said. "If necessary I can prove that the empty shell I found from where you fired the shot came from your rifle, and I can show a jury the tree you were up in when you fired the shot. The neighbor's house just happened to come into line when you shot at that running deer."

"I'll be darned," said Peter. "Are you sure that there is absolutely no way that I might not have been the shooter?"

"Only if someone else was shooting your gun, and I highly doubt that," I said. "Listen, I'm going to mail you a summons for the offense of reckless use of a fire arm. That's less than care-less use, which can more than likely involve jail time," I said. "I'm also not going to charge you for hunting from the tree. I know they're trying to make it legal to hunt from tree stands with rifles, but it's still illegal to rifle hunt from a raised platform."

"I appreciate that," Said Peter. "Can I handle this by mail?

"Yes you can," I answered. "Normally I'd ask the judge to require you to appear in person. Let him chew on your ear for a while. But I think you've learned your lesson, and you'll be more careful in the future."

"Thanks. Is there some way I can contact the family and apologize?" he asked.

"Let me tell them that you're sorry," I answered. "I'm not sure that you're making contact with the man of the house right now would be a good thing."

Robin Harrington smiled as I explained the investigation and arrest. He had naturally calmed down considerably since the incident. "Thanks for all you did," he said. "As far as I'm concerned he's lucky he didn't go to jail."

"Well, he made a stupid mistake," I said. "Jail won't fix 'stu-pid', and if I felt for a minute that he was the habitually careless kind, he'd have gone to jail. I'm going to caution your neighbor about over booking his deer hunts, and impress a few safety tips on him as well."

I handed Robin the bullet that had nearly ended his daugh-ter's life. "Here, give this to Maria. She may want to put it in a locket someday. Tell her I said for her to keep training for cross country. I know you feel that the fellow who shot your house is lucky about not going to jail. But Maria? Now there's one lucky lady!"

No Matter Which
Way You Turn

"Eight-nine from two one-thirty-one, in service."

"We're clear, two one-thirty-one. Kind of early aren't you?" Happy Harold's voice sounded groggy. After forty years on the force I couldn't fault the tough street cop sergeant at the Stephenson State Police post one bit for putting his feet up and catching a late grave yard shift nap.

"Not really. Been up since four AM. Maintenance day. Headed for Escanaba."

"We got you on the log. Have a safe trip," said Harold. One could only imagine him reaching for the now stale coffee pot to jog his spirits for the upcoming shift change.

My day had started two hours earlier. I had retrieved the department's twenty-one foot Glastron patrol boat from the storage garage in the town of Norway the day before. Now I was too excited to sleep and had gone to my heated shop to start pre-season maintenance on the boat. Lifting the engine cover I was dismayed to discover clear water dripping down the side of the Ford 351 engine. Ice crystals on the oil dipstick confirmed my fears. Someone had neglected to winterize the boat last fall, causing the engine cooling system to freeze solid, cracking the block and ruining the motor.

This development would mean writing a full report to the district supervisor, a circular firing squad of blame shifting, and the search for a new and very expensive engine. Being on the bottom of the pecking order, I was certain that the blame would fall on me, but that's a different story. Maybe I could arrange for a good used engine from our local salvage yard and gain a few brownie points; at least enough to bring me back up to 'empty' on the good graces scale in the district.

No time to worry about that. I could spend the next few hours installing the Sheriff's department radio in the boat. It was an old model, half vacuum tubes and half transistor, but it was a one hundred watt, nearly bullet proof model. VCO Nate and I had picked up many road killed fur bearing animals the previous fall while on patrol; their pelts sold by Nate to raise funds to purchase the radio from a local radio repair shop. The term "radio coon" was used to describe such roadside finds.

After an hour of drilling, placing, changing, and wiring I was ready to test the radio. Turning the knob to "on" I was greeted by absolute silence and a blank set of lights which should have sprung to life, heralding a joyous rebirth of radio capabilities. Lifting the cover from the main radio box I could see a number of connections in various stages of corrosion. No outgoing messages for this puppy today. A visit to the radio hospital was in order, so all the wiring and fastening was undone. Maybe I should just take a road trip and pick up that snow mobile trailer that district three had bequeathed to district two.

Turning east onto highway G-12 my spirits were lifted by a rosy false dawn, promising a bright, sunny day. A light coating of early spring frost on the blacktop served to slow my otherwise hurried progress toward the town of Cedar River.

Once on highway M-35 the near absence of traffic and dry

pavement made travel enjoyable. Skeins of thousands of some sort of insect drifted skyward from the apex of the many cedar trees lining the highway, giving the illusion of rising smoke. At Fox Park I stopped to view a glorious sunrise. You just can't beat daybreak at Deer Creek. The brief span of the fifteen minutes spent enjoying the sun breaking the horizon could have yielded a hundred pictures; each one different, and each one almost unbearably beautiful. Thank you, Lord. Time to move on.

Arriving at the District Three office I was greeted by the local sergeant who directed me to the 'gift' snow mobile trailer in the back lot. I have always been told to beware of Greeks bearing gifts, and to never buy a used bulldozer. However being one to never pass up anything free, I was overjoyed to hook onto this somewhat 'used' trailer, anticipating the short project of getting it back up and in service for district two.

I should have been tipped off with the discovery that the tongue of this trailer had no 'innards' to the ball hitch. There should be a locking device that snaps shut, securing the trailer to the ball hitch of the car. With these parts missing I merrily set about wrapping twenty or so layers of black plastic electrician's tape around the tongue at the rear of the ball hitch, tying the tongue more or less snugly to the patrol car's ball hitch. Don't worry about whether or not the lights work; we won't be traveling slow enough to have a rear end collision on the way home. A quick look at the tires and we're off.

All went well until the straight stretch just south of No Seeum creek. Looking back I noticed that the trailer appeared to be sagging to the right, and that the trailer was riding in a rather rough fashion. Of course this meant a flat trailer tire on the passenger side, but I was prepared with a spare in the trunk of the patrol car.

Although the lug nuts were rusted, making changing the tire difficult, the task was completed with the breaking of only one lug bolt.

Back on the road things went quite smoothly until the

crossing of the county line. The trailer seemed to be dragging to starboard, and wisps of gray smoke emanated from the right side of the trailer. Pulling over and investigating I discovered that the wheel bearing had disintegrated, the dust cap having vibrated off and several flat sided bearings fell out as the tire was rotated slowly.

Searching the trunk of the patrol car I retrieved a quart of 10W-40 motor oil, poured as much of the thick liquid as the bearing cavity would hold, and limped home on the shoulder of the highway.

Pulling into the yard I noticed that the fuel gauge was reading 'empty', making a trip necessary to Stephenson for fuel.

Big Ben was working day shift at the State police post, and his cheery greeting was most welcome to my somewhat somber mood, thus rendered by the morning's events.

Good old friend Ben, master of the situational catch phrase, listened attentively as I recounted the events of the previous eight hours. At the end of my story his assessment was as could be expected. "Sounds like a nice piece of equipment. Shouldn't cost a whole lot more than a brand new trailer to fix. Sorry about all the work it took to get it. I've had those days, too. Sometimes no matter which way you turn your behind is behind you."

"Your behind is behind you..." I ruminated. "Not bad philosophy. I'd have to be careful where I used it. How long have you been waiting to use that line?"

"Just now thought it up, although I was thinking of a more crass, earthy term for 'behind', but I'm actually trying to clean up my language. Yeah you're right, you'd have to watch it. Women who have big behinds usually live longer than men who mention it."

That was enough of Big Ben. I was still laughing as I drove away, but not for long. A mile east of Stephenson the patrol car's engine began to miss. Within several miles the car was bucking and smoking profusely. Thankfully the engine continued to run until the car was safely in my driveway, where it stalled.

The phone was ringing as I opened the front door. It was Ben. "Hey guy, did you get some gas when you were here? I see you entered sixteen gallons in the gas log."

"Yessir I did, Ben, and I think that might be my problem. Is there something wrong with your gas supply?"

"Not a thing pal, except that it's all diesel fuel. The gas company filled us up this morning and put in the wrong fuel. We just now found it out. Maybe you can have your car towed and repaired."

"Don't worry about it Ben. Remember, I'm a certified master mechanic. I'll just siphon out the tank and bleed the fuel system. But you're right. Sometimes no matter which way you turn....."

Harvest Time

The year was 1979. Spring was threatening to arrive late as the snow banks began to finally melt in mid-March. The gradually warming westerly winds brought their seasonal runoffs, swelling the recently ice coated streams to nearly over-flowing, turning their waters to a muddy chocolate brown.

Currents ran cold and swift, making conditions much too hostile for Northern Pike to commence their journeys from Green Bay up the creeks for their annual spawning run. With the waters in their present state only a few adventurous Trout would be enticed up the icy streams and the Pike would just have to wait another week until the waters subsided and warmed considerably. Or would they?

The mercury hovered at thirty degrees as CO Tom and I cruised south of Cedar River on Highway M-35. The day had been a warm one, the temperature rising into the mid-forties, dipping back to below freezing just after nightfall; typical for March weather. The overnight freeze would tighten the soil, slowing the runoff and lowering the creeks slightly.

As usual, Tom and I could not wait for the spring fish runs to begin. Winter with its snowmobile and ice fishing patrols had kept us in its grip for long enough. We were more than ready to get back out on foot patrol in some lighter clothing; hence our "jump the gun" early fish run scouting.

As we approached Beattie creek we noticed an older model, light green Dodge sedan parked in the driveway of an unoccupied summer home on the west side of the highway. Thinking it to be a possible burglary of the residence we drove south of the creek, parking a short distance down a brushy logging trail. With portable radios in hand we then began our stalk back north to the old green car.

Our quest was curtailed as we crossed the bridge in the darkness with the discovery of lights along the south bank of Beattie creek, down near the Bay. At the sound of an approaching car the lights extinguished, coming back on after the car had passed. More than likely these were our people with the old car parked to the north.

Concealing ourselves in the lilac thickets on the north side of the stream, Tom and I observed the actions of the spot lighters and were amazed at what we saw. The four individuals were slowly wading upstream, carefully shining the water as they approached. Not your usual sportsmen, they were dressed like genuine old time homestead farmers. Olive green rubber barn boots, bib overalls, tattered plaid wool jackets and corduroy ear lopper hats made up the compliment of their dress. Instead of multi-tined spears they carried three tined pitchforks! Burlap feed sacks were carried to hold their catch, which Tom and I thought would be little to nothing.

Instead of the popular high candle powered spotlights used by contemporary sportsmen our farmers were using old style two cell incandescent flash lights which they used most judiciously, being careful to turn them off at the slightest sound, only switching them on once all threat of a passing vehicle or noise back in the brush had passed.

One of the group would use his light to shine along the stream bank while another would gently prod under the bank with the tines of the fork. Amazingly they were catching a great number of fish! The rushing water was deep enough so as to occasionally run over the tops of the barn boots. To this the poachers paid little heed. No words were spoken; no shouts of glee should a particularly large Pike or Trout be impaled. The fish was merely lifted from the water and dropped into a waiting burlap bag.

Tom and I watched in rapt silence. Never before had we witnessed such successful or efficient poaching. All fish were kept, from a small sixteen inch "hammer handle" Pike to one nearly thirty four inches in length. Obviously these folks lived a "waste not, want not" life style.

Soon the group had reached the property line fence at the highway. Traversing the ditch bank, they hiked north along the roadside to their old green car.

Tom and I followed at a discreet distance, prepared to dive into the roadside grass should the approach of a vehicle threaten to give away our presence. The trunk was opened and three gunny sacks of fish were deposited into an interior already cluttered with tools, loops of bailer twine and more feed sacks. The smallest of the four men reached into a bag of fish, removed a silvery Rainbow Trout and began to admire its iridescent colors.

"Put it back in the bag Robin," said one of the older two. "We can look at them later. We have to watch for the Game Warden."

"Oh, don't be so scared," said Robin. "They're so dumb, they don't even know what to look for."

"Evening gents," I said. "Did you have any luck?"

The trunk lid was instantly slammed and the surprised group jumped back like kids caught in a cookie jar. "We're just not doing anything!" exclaimed Robin, searching for words, any words to somehow help them out of their situation.

Identification was taken from all four, two of whom were juvenile offenders. Otto, the owner of the car, was allowed to drive the vehicle to the Menominee county jail while Tom and I transported the remaining three men in the patrol car. All were charged with the illegal taking of sport fish. The fish, of which there were nearly eighty pounds were confiscated, and the old green car retained as evidence. According to policy, the car was inventory searched. Along with the tools, porcelain fence insulators, old nails and chaff, the car held the comfortable odor of the old style twelve cow dairy barns of many years past, reminiscent of my childhood days.

All four were Wisconsin residents, making it necessary for the two adults to post a bond before being released. Charges against the two juveniles were dismissed and the adults ordered by the court to pay $10.00 per pound for the sport fish, as well a fine for the offense of taking sport fish illegally.

I do not know how these fellows knew that the muddy, raging Beattie Creek held an early run of Pike and Trout that night. Nor have I ever before witnessed such a casual, quiet, efficient method of poaching spring run fish.

It appears to me that their excursion was just another aspect of their simple farming life. In June you put up hay. In late August you harvest wheat. In February you butcher the hogs. In mid-March just go out and get some spring run fish to pickle and can. At no time during the arrest was there any resistance or argument given. It was as if that was just another possible outcome of this type of harvest. Take life as it comes. Sometimes you eat the Bear; sometimes the Bear eats you.

The fines were eventually paid and the old green car returned to its owner. I don't believe that the State ever retrieved full compensation for the fish. But I do believe that our purpose was served. We never encountered them back on any of the Green Bay streams. At least from these simple living, honest farmers, the fish were safe.

I Wanna Rock and Roll

Nearly every police department in the country, no matter how specialized, has had to deal with some aspect of the consumption of alcohol by underage adolescents. In the case of the conservation officer it involves the enforcement of littering and land use laws along with statutes concerning the minimum drinking age and driving under the influence.

Each department has its own written or unwritten policies for handling cases involving teenage drinking. While safety is of utmost importance, a majority of police officers are reluctant to charge youngsters with violations that could adversely affect their futures. Cases of drunk driving are usually dealt with seriously, but teenage drinking parties are often discouraged by mere officer presence in the area and very visible drive-by's through the neighborhood.

Drinking parties in the State Forest or at State Forest campgrounds are usually encountered by Conservation Officers rather than State or local police agencies. The presence of such a party is often evidenced by a preponderance of vehicle tracks into a forested area or the number of empty beer cans strewn along county roads leading to the site.

One common method of breaking up a drinking party is to drive into the site with lights flashing and sirens blowing, scattering the group into the woods. The officers then talk with any occupants remaining at the site, usually writing very few or no citations due to the paucity of remaining suspects, and then depart, confident that they have done their job. This method more often than not simply results in the underage teens moving their party to another site and continuing their festivities.

One practice which I have found to be very effective is to conceal the patrol car a distance away from the party and walk in. Observing from a distance, it can be noted who is in possession of the drinks. After a short period of time the officer quietly walks into the site and makes his presence known. Very few people, if any, run away, but will often drop their drinks on the ground. Identifications are then collected and those who have dropped or thrown their drinks are asked if they plan to pick them up. The common answer is "no", denying that they possessed the cup or can. Littering tickets are then issued. It's a minor civil infraction, easily paid without a criminal record, and the litterbug will probably not commit the violation again in the near future. If the provider of the alcohol can be determined, they are dealt with more severely. Often any remaining alcohol is poured out on the ground in lieu of criminal charges of possession. The emptying of a keg of beer can cause many a groan of disappointment. Sometimes the sheer volume of the libation lost by the revelers can cause distress of biblical proportions.

"Sultry" would be the word used to describe that August night in 1987 when VCO Nate and myself wheeled into the Big Cedar River state forest campground. The air conditioning was condensing the humidity at such a rapid rate that the windshield kept fogging and it was necessary to occasionally run the wipers.

Dousing the parking lights and pulling into campsite number two we were somewhat surprised at the total absence of campfires at nearby sites. Stepping from the patrol car we were met with a rush of hot humid air. Not a single star shone in the overcast sky and the hemlock trees dripped with moisture. Crickets supplied the only woodland sound. The campground appeared to be completely empty.

"Wow, it's blacker than the inside of a cow," said Nate. "No sense walking around, getting sweatier. Let's get back inside the car where it's nice."

We were just in the process of re-entering the car when suddenly our ears were accosted with the sound of piercing, loud, heavy metal rock music emanating from down by the river in the walk in sites. Something about wanting to rock and roll all through the night and all the next day. The walk in sites had recently been opened to vehicles and were concealed by the heavy cedar trees out on a small peninsula surrounded by the river.

"Well now, that changes things!" exclaimed Nate. "Time to saddle up!"

The two young men sitting at the picnic table on campsite 32 could have been named Dick Decent and Todd Trueheart. The clean cut pair looked the epitome of your stereotype All American Boys. Except for the blaring hard rock and the half consumed bottle of whiskey between them.

Reaching into the open window of their red short box pickup to turn off the sound I greeted them and asked for their identification. The startled pair produced their driver's licenses, revealing them both to under the legal drinking age.

"Guys, you haven't registered your camp, and you're too young to have alcohol. I will be citing you for failing to pay the camping fee, but I'll give you a break on the more serious alcohol violation by just having you pour the remaining whiskey on the ground." I said.

"Oh, sure, no problem," said the blonde haired, taller of the two boys.

The more diminutive of the pair sported close cropped, bright red hair. Picking up the bottle he carried it to the cedar fence at the edge of the campsite, poured the alcohol over the river bank and returned with the empty bottle.

Calling me aside, Nate quietly said "Something isn't right here. Those two are way too happy to dump out half a bottle of good whiskey. They want us to write the ticket and leave. There is more to this than we think."

Off to the north side of the site, in the shadows, sat a small utility trailer with wooden sides, covered by a tarp. It could have been assumed that this trailer held camping equipment. A peek under the canvass revealed twenty four, (count 'em), twenty four cases of beer!

"Fellas, what are you up to?!" I exclaimed. "Surely you don't plan to drink all of this!" Not one word from the guilty pair. There would be no explanation from these boys as to their plans for all the suds.

"Okay, here's the deal," I said. "I'm not going to go back on my word. You have the option of pouring out each and every bottle and I'll let it go with a warning."

"Naw! Ya can't do this to us man!" Blondie's Boy Scout English suddenly took on a street vernacular accent. "This is BOGUE man!"

The boy with the red hair began to grouse as well "Man, if this was Marquette, not one thing would be said about it!"

"I seriously doubt you my friend, but okay, you don't have to dump the beer. I'll just go by the book, confiscate all this evidence, and we'll go see the judge."

"No, no, no...We'll dump it all out," Both boys began unloading the cases and opening the bottles.

Half an hour later there were two sets of blistered hands and the strong odor of beer about the campsite. Both boys appeared as if their entire year had been ruined. We presented them the citation for illegal camping and bade them good evening.

Pulling out from the mile long campground road onto highway 551 we were met by three cars. As the vehicles slowed to make the turn into the road our sweeping headlights revealed the three cars to be full of smiling young adults, more than likely headed for campsite number 32.

After several minutes of quietly cruising along Nate broke the silence. "Guess someone won't be rockin' and rollin' tonight!"

It's a Decoy!

Menominee County has long been noted for its large population of Whitetail Deer. Mild winters and large scale dairy farming provided the ideal climate and forage for these animals, causing the county to have the highest number of deer in Michigan's Upper Peninsula. Because of the damage to dairy crops and high number of car/deer accidents this was a mixed blessing. Deer hunters would inundate the county during the rifle deer season with a sea of bright orange. Both farmers and auto insurance companies were happy to have the deer numbers reduced and local businesses appreciated the economic boost. However with the hunters came problems as well.

In an effort to reduce the high numbers of deer, Michigan DNR biologists relaxed the regulations on the number of deer that could be taken by hunters in the form of extra kill tags issued if a hunter were to bring in his deer for registration. Information concerning the age, sex, and condition of the deer would be taken, and an additional kill tag for an antlerless deer supplied to the hunter enabling him to take yet another deer. Farmers were also issued "Block permits" which they could give to guests who were hunting on their property, enabling them to take even more animals.

Over all this program worked quite well. However as with anything of which there is a surplus, the deer decreased in value and many hunters forgot the use of safety, common sense and good manners. Hunters would journey to Menominee County with several deer tags in possession but have no property upon which to hunt. Finding State land overcrowded and unable to get permission from landowners who were already hosting hunters, these sportsmen often cruised the side roads in search of deer which they would shoot from the windows of their vehicles. This highly unsafe and illegal practice is known as "Road hunting". Indeed hunters often came to the county for the express purpose of road hunting with no thought in mind of seeking permission to hunt.

Trespassing went hand in hand with road hunting and many complaints were answered and numerous citations for trespassing issued. One trio of hunters were apprehended while dragging a deer from a farmer's field past a "No trespassing" sign. "Look," said one of the three. "We're really sorry. All we wanted to do is come down here, throw six deer on the car, and go back home. We really didn't want any trouble." Compare that with thirty years in the past when one hunter in seven felt lucky to bag a deer.

By the mid 1980's road hunting had become a serious problem. Accidents involving the discharge of a firearm in automobile are one of the most common causes of hunting fatalities. Several close calls during previous seasons highlighted the need for concerted enforcement efforts in this area. One landowner who was sitting in his deer blind watched a vehicle stop along the road across the field from his deer bind and shoot at several deer between them. The bullet missed the deer, but came through the deer blind, shooting the landowner's hat from his head. Another road hunter shot a hole through his right foot, and another lost his life when a bullet severed his femoral artery. In the name of responsible law enforcement, something had to be done.

Successful game law enforcement can be described as a triangle. There is the poacher, the conservation officer, and the wild game. In order for an arrest to be made and the poacher stopped, all three elements must be present. Often there would be game in an opportune location such as a remote field, and there would be a poacher, but no officer. Sometimes there would be a concealed officer watching a would-be poacher, but no game would be present. Bringing all three elements together was extremely difficult, and routine mobile patrol was not deterrent enough to reduce the violations significantly.

At the 1986 Michigan and Wisconsin Border officers' meeting an answer to road hunting enforcement was presented. Wisconsin Conservation Officers had begun using a decoy in the form of a full body mounted deer which they would place in a safe location where a road hunter would be likely to shoot at it. The officers would then conceal themselves and make an arrest should a road hunter attempt to shoot the decoy. The State of Wisconsin had experienced a good degree of success with the program and I suggested to our district supervisor that we look into the possibility of starting our own decoy program. The district supervisor was doubtful that the chief of our division would be receptive, citing entrapment and the possibility of lawsuits as obstacles to be overcome.

As the weeks and months passed I would periodically touch bases with my lieutenant, asking if any progress had been made in the direction of a decoy program becoming a reality. The answer was always the same, that the Lansing office considered the use of a decoy to be entrapment. I would answer that we wouldn't be doing anything to tempt an honest citizen to break the law any more than the temptation offered by naturally occurring game. We would merely be bringing all three parts of the triangle together in a safe location in an effort to make hunting a safer sport. Finally, I believe more than anything, to get rid of my persistence, I was told that if full body mount of a wild turkey could be obtained in time for the upcoming turkey season, we could start a pilot program. The decoy would be set out and the resulting violations videotaped to show Lansing the extent of our road hunting problem. The mounted turkey could not cost over thirty dollars.

Anyone who has any knowledge of taxidermy knows that no wild turkey mounts of any kind can be had for under thirty dollars. The cost would be several hundred dollars and I was sure that the thought from the Lansing office was that I would have to abandon my quest, unable to accomplish this impossible task.

Undeterred, I visited a local taxidermist and good friend, Harold DeYoung. Buddy, as he was called, managed a small family zoo and was always receptive to taking in orphaned or confiscated animals, and through the years Buddy and I had become good friends. My plan was to visit Buddy and in the course of conversation mention the decoy program and see if perhaps some road killed turkey hides stretched around an excelsior body might make for a passible facsimile of a wild turkey. We had been making small talk for several minutes when Buddy said, "Hey, come on in the other room. I have something to show you."

There in the middle of his taxidermy room stood a large, beautiful mounted tom turkey; a trophy which he had shot the season prior. The turkey had weighed twenty one pounds. This was the perfect time to bring up the possibility of throwing some sort of jury rigged decoy together. Before I could say a word I was nearly knocked off my feet by Buddy's next suggestion:

"Hey, why don't you take it and set it out in a field along the road. Just see how many people shoot at it." Goodness me! There *is* a God!

"Gosh no Buddy, this is your beautiful trophy. I couldn't do that."

"Sure you can! I'll get another turkey this season; they're all over the woods here. You take this and have fun with it. I bet you'll catch a lot of bad guys!"

"Well thanks a million Buddy. I'm sure we'll end up naming him 'Buddy.'"

Numb with disbelief I drove home on a cloud of victory with "Buddy" sitting up proudly in the rear seat of the patrol car. While my lieutenant was aghast with disbelief he was equally enthused and eager to get the project started. One point upon which we disagreed was that I felt we should arrest any poachers that we witnessed illegally shooting the decoy, as the arrests would be part of the real program should it be sanctioned. We would have to know the degree of difficulty in apprehending the miscreants, including chasing them down and stopping them. The lieutenant was unmoved. We were to videotape only, and that was that.

The early morning sun was just easing over the horizon as Sergeant Bart, Lieutenant Kirk, and myself concealed the patrol car in an abandoned garage adjacent to a clover field bordering an oak forest. Buddy had been set up in the field approximately twenty yards from the road side with large "No Trespassing" signs fifty feet on either side. The video camera was readied and aimed at the decoy some thirty yards to the west.

Buddy enjoyed his life as an unscathed decoy for just under six minutes. The next vehicle to drive by contained two fellows in full camo clothing. The pickup truck drove to the next intersection, sped back to the decoy and "BAM"; the shotgun barrel from the passenger's window sent lead shot, flame and smoke in Buddy's direction. Buddy lurched sideways from the impact of the blast. Sensing that something was amiss when the bird did not fall over or fly away the driver sped off, tires squealing.

I had not taken into account the adrenaline rush that would go with witnessing someone shooting at the decoy just as we had planned. The hunters were out there to break the law and we had arranged conditions so that they committed the violation in front of us. Kirk and Bart were furiously pounding me on the shoulders: "GO! GO! GO! GET 'EM! GET 'EM!" All thoughts of merely videotaping the violations were instantly out the window. The law had been broken and they wanted me to go run those boys down. Sergeant Bart nearly had his foot slammed in the car door as he jumped into my departing patrol car.

The pickup was stopped within a mile of the decoy and both hunters were more surprised than pleased to be informed that they were the very first road hunters to face the wrath of Buddy the decoy. Citations were issued for hunting from a motor vehicle and the case was concluded without incident.

Buddy went on to take part in some fifty or more arrests. The public accepted the decoy program as a tool to make hunting season safer, and road hunting indeed decreased by a noticeable amount. A few detractors attempted to cry "foul play" or "Entrapment", but the explanation that firearm safety is not a game usually quelled most complaints.

At first a small segment of the news media attempted to portray conservation officers as watching the videos of people shooting the decoys, rolling on the floor amid raucous gales of laughter. The problem of road hunting was certainly no laughing matter, nor was the partial solution offered by the decoy program. Although sometimes we did enjoy some truly humorous situations as the following stories will reveal.

During the first day of Buddy's debut we observed a Stephenson school bus which drove past our location several times on its assigned route. At approximately one in the afternoon two women rode up on a four wheeler carrying a twenty two rifle. They stopped the ORV, stepped off and the driver pointed the rifle at the decoy. She then put the gun down (it was not loaded) and tried to shoo the decoy away. Failing this she walked over to the garage and attempted to tear a board off the building, obviously planning to whack the decoy with the board.

We felt it necessary to make ourselves known in the interest of Buddy's safety so we stepped out and surprised the pair. The driver explained that she had thought the decoy to have been wounded by road hunters, having observed the bird every time she had driven by in the school bus. She felt it necessary to put the poor bird out of its suffering. No charges were filed of course, but she was told that the video would be held for blackmail should it ever be necessary.

Buddy DeYoung built a number of decoys in the following seasons including several deer in standing and lying positions. The deer decoys had several sets of antlers that could be screwed in to alter the appearance of the deer to be an antlerless deer, spike horn, or trophy buck. On one decoy I had placed a model airplane servo beneath the tail, hooked to the tail so that remote control could be used to wag the tail in a realistic manner.

One young taxidermist had been talking around town that a person would really have to be dumb to be fooled by a mounted deer. This same individual was also rumored to have done a little hunting himself from the window of a pickup truck. He had vowed that when he encountered the deer decoy being deployed he would spend the afternoon giving us the 'raspberries', and warning other hunters

As it occurred one Sunday afternoon during the rifle season two other officers and I had decided to try out the new reposing buck along with the doe whose tail would wag. During the afternoon we witnessed several "Good bets" who might have taken a shot but were too wary. Then along came our taxidermist. Two wags of the tail and the hook was set. Out came the rifle and "bang!" went the gun. Our taxidermist and his partner actually stood around laughing about getting caught. They had to be asked to move on as we were beginning to draw a crowd. From then on his line was "I've seen *real* deer that didn't look as good as that buck!"

Another time the decoy buck was set up a few miles west of the village of Wallace. A pickup truck drove by, saw the decoy and stopped. The driver stepped out of the truck, removed his cased rifle, loaded it, raised it to aim at the deer, then lowered the rifle, unloaded it and drove off. Curiosity overcame the officers and they pursued the truck to ask why he had not shot. Upon stopping, Buddy DeYoung stepped from the vehicle. He had nearly been caught by his own decoy! There would have been no violation as the rifle was not loaded in the truck and he had permission to hunt the land where the decoy had been set up. It certainly spoke well of Buddy's work.

One individual whom I have thoroughly enjoyed through the years was a businessman by the name of Rick Bradshaw. Rick was always too busy to bother with a little thing like the law. For a number of years I would arrest him at least once per season on some violation such as hunting deer with a spotlight or possessing a loaded firearm in a motor vehicle. We actually became quite good friends though more than once we faced each other in court. Upon being arrested Rick would always complain," This is wrong, man! Last year, yeah, okay you had me fair and square. But this here is bogus!"

The next year he would complain about the new citation, but he always paid the fine, one way or another. When word of the decoy spread around Rick began asking me to show him the deer decoy. "Show me the dummy deer! I want to be able to know what it looks like so I won't get caught."

Of course I did most certainly not show him the "dummy", knowing that sooner or later his turn would come.

The second to last day of deer season was not the type of cold, rainy day that one would relish, sitting in a brush pile along the road, waiting for some road hunter to take the bait. Nevertheless VCO Nate had volunteered to be the observer while I sat, concealed in a nearby valley with the patrol car at the ready.

At two PM the radio crackled to life. "We got a good bet," Said Nate. "He's really rolling by slow. He's stopped. OH-OH! He just shot!"

The patrol car roared to life and I shot up the two track road, swerving onto the gravel side road as the big grey Olds Tornado sped by. The car did not stop until the passenger had fully unloaded the rifle; the movements of which I could see through the back window of the Olds. Once the vehicle rolled to a stop I ran up to the sedan, shaking hands with Rick Bradshaw as he stepped from the car. "Well dang it, ya got me!" exclaimed Rick. He introduced his friend from California sitting in the passenger seat with the uncased rifle and cartridges strewn about. "Sorry about shooting the horns off the deer. I only take head shots and I instructed my friend to do the same," said Rick, unknowingly implicating his friend as well as himself. "It was worth it. At least now I know what the dummy looks like."

"So do I." said the friend from California pointing to Rick.

The decoy program is now used statewide and many improvements have been made. The decoys are even more lifelike with some of them able to move their heads. Modern technology has made it easier and better, but maybe taken some of the old time fun out of it as well.

One spring afternoon in 2008 I visited the State Police/DNR station prior to moving downstate. Retrieving some of my old property made it necessary to climb the stairs to the second floor storage area. At the top of the stairs I stopped, momentarily surprised by what I saw. There in the corner stood Buddy the Turkey. Wires held up what was left of his tail. He had been mended many times. Numerous BB holes pocked the painted plastic head of this once proud instrument of road hunter justice. He was obviously too far gone to be used as a decoy any more.

As the memories of all those happy days gone down flooded back, I thought "Well played old boy. Rest in peace".

Kids on the River

Sometime in the mid 1980's our family became involved with a 4H sponsored club known simply as 'Challenge". This group was formed in an effort to provide area youth with opportunities to learn about outdoor activities and skills such as survival, rock climbing, canoeing, camping, hiking, and kayaking. Many other activities were included such as kayak construction, building of outdoor shelters, and outdoor cuisine. Camping and canoeing trips were scheduled any time enough instructors and kids could be gathered to form a group of 6 or more participants.

In the beginning a number of volunteer instructors were schooled in the skills and philosophy of Challenge. As an instructor in canoeing and camping I worked closely with Wayne Mulzer, a retired Air Force meteorologist who had an affinity for children and a special desire to teach them the skills they would need to survive in today's world. From the very beginning Wayne and I worked hand in glove, and before long we were as close as brothers.

Both Wayne and I enjoyed canoeing and at every opportunity we would head for the water with a group of young
Challenge members. At times we discovered the river to be
too low, or perhaps too high and would have to cancel the trip.
More often than not we would have an alternate stream in mind
and merely switch locations for our voyage. Our trips generally
involved an afternoon; rarely more than four hours. Overnight
camping trips sometimes involved the use of canoes, which
made the camping all the more enjoyable.

From ice-out in the spring until my law enforcement duties
called me away during the autumn I would endeavor to participate in as many canoe trips as possible because, well, they
were fun for me, too.

One early spring morning I answered the phone as I was walking out the door on the way to church. It was Wayne asking if I
could join a group that afternoon running the Menominee
River from White Rapids down to the old Shakey Lakes State
forest campground. The river was still high from spring runoff,
but most of the ice was out. Of course I said "yes!"

At one PM we met on the shore below the White Rapids
dam. The launching went smoothly and the paddling was easy
as the swift spring currents propelled us downstream. All we
had to do was steer, which was good for honing the paddling
skills of our new members. Drifting through the river valley
was a pleasant experience as the spring afternoon sun reflected off the crystal clear riffles. Then, as we rounded a curve
immediately above a deep stretch of river known as "The
Sturgeon Hole" we were shocked to see that we were fast approaching an ice jam.

Sheets of ice as thick as one foot had been drifting down-
river from as far as one hundred miles upstream. Normally
this pack ice moves harmlessly along on its journey to Green
Bay in Lake Michigan. Occasionally a large sheet will hang up

on a mid-stream boulder or log, causing the following ice to "jam" behind it, creating flooding conditions and many dangerous, unpredictable currents around it. Any water craft coming into upstream contact with a jam would tend to turn sideways against the jam and the current running under the craft would capsize it, spilling the occupants into the raging waters and under the ice pack to drown in the icy water. It was into one such large ice jam that our small group was heading.

Pulling a hard left rudder I began to paddle furiously to the east shore, shouting to the others to do the same. Four of our six boat group gained shore above the jam. Two canoes ran into the ice fifty some yards out into the river. My heart was in my throat, expecting so see one or both canoes capsize at any moment. As their craft swung around parallel to the jam Wayne and I shouted "Paddle! Paddle! Paddle". By some good providence both canoes separated from the ice and began a slow trip to shore.

Once all souls were safely ashore we were greeted with another problem. Before us stood a large "No trespassing", sign accompanied by another that read "Trespassers will be prosecuted to the fullest extent of the law". The owner of this property had a reputation for strictly enforcing his property posting. Hopefully the landowner, if present, would understand the situation and not view our presence as a typical trespassing incident.

As if on cue, our landowner opened the back door of his cabin and walked down to meet us on the shore. "Oh, so that's what all the shouting was about," he said. By now I was already formulating some sort of 'plan B', whereby we would have to walk our canoes back upstream half a mile or so and take out on more friendly ground, cutting our canoe trip short and spending a lot of time contacting our pickup cars.

"Wow!" said George the landowner. "That could have been dicey. People have died getting swept under an ice jam. Well, let's get you guys up across my lawn and back into the river down there where it's safe."

That was totally unexpected. Gratefully we accepted his offer of assistance and portaged the canoes, continuing our voyage on what remained of a most pleasant afternoon. Once a good distance downstream Wayne pulled his canoe close to mine. "I didn't know just what was going to transpire back there. I knew that you and George haven't always been on the best of terms. He could have made it tough for us."

Maybe it was because I had given George several breaks in the past. Maybe it was because he recognized that we were out teaching our county's youth valuable life qualities. Or maybe, as I replied to Wayne, "We're both professionals."

Years have passed and Wayne and I are too old and tired to spend much time in a canoe, or to sleep in many more snow banks, but the memories remain as clear as the days when we lived them. If it were possible to go back in time, my choice would be to get back into the canoes and paddle down the mighty Menominee, spending an afternoon with kids on the river.

‿✿‿

Nature's Engineers

One of the most unique and beloved animals on God's good earth is the North American Beaver. These small woodland creatures fit right in when it comes to depicting wildlife in a positive manner. Soft and furry, compact and cute, beavers are often the stars of animated cartoons and wildlife documentaries. Cartoon artists usually give them catchy names like "Billy" or "Buddy". They feature them wearing little hard hats as they waddle around solving problems and help those in need, usually saving the day in some energetic, ingenious way. Millions have been made by wildlife photographers making movies of these engineers of the wild as they construct dams, chew off trees, and conduct other various projects sure to change the course of history. Equipped by nature with a perpetually optimistic facial expression, it goes without saying that they are all good spirited individuals. No one has ever met an angry, evil beaver. Their sharp teeth, dexterous paws and flat tail equip them to meet any challenge; solve any problem.

Beavers have evolved throughout time and have adapted to function in an ever changing world. Many years ago beavers were the size of small horses and probably required more food and larger houses to exist. When continents shifted and climate changed many animal species became extinct along with the dinosaurs. The beaver, however, grew smaller, faster and smarter, changing right along with the environment; securing its place in modern day life. They continue to adapt from animals of the deep forest into survivors in streams, rivers and lakes right in our back yards. Living in close proximity to humans, beavers can become quite tame if left unmolested and will often keep right on working while being observed at a distance by curious onlookers. People are fascinated by the energy and ingenuity as they repair the dam, cut trees, and gather food. They are indeed, fun to watch. When a sudden shout or clap of the hands causes them to smack their tails on the surface of the pond and dive below, well, that's fun to watch, too.

In the wilderness beavers build ideal wildlife habitat with the ponds created by their dams. The purpose of the dam from the viewpoint of the beavers is simple. They need the water to surround their houses, creating a moat around these hollowed out piles of sticks and mud to prevent attacks by predators. Water also facilitates the transportation of tree branches used for food and construction. The spinoff benefits are many. The miniature lakes make ideal habitat for brook trout and other fish. Muskrats, waterfowl, turtles and other aquatic species thrive in these wetlands. Predators such as Eagles, hawks, bobcats, and coyotes are attracted to these wildlife havens and a good time is had by all. Upon discovering that beavers have set up housekeeping in the small creek traversing private property the owners are usually delighted, in the beginning.

"Hey John, come on over and see the new beaver dam in our woods," might be the greeting of a new beaver dam recipient.

"Oh. Are they damming up your trout stream?"

"Yeah. It's really neat! We're going to have a trout pond and everything. I can't wait until it fills up." The term is usually "Our beavers", and no one had better mess with them.

Six months later it is noticed that approximately forty acres of prime aspen or cedar forest has been flooded by the pond and all the trees are dying. The upstream farmer can no longer cross the small bridge to his hay fields and the water surrounding his road is turning the roadbed to mush. Now these former delightful, cute animals become the "DNR's Beavers", and complaints requesting the removal of the pesky buggers come rolling in.

Ideally the best way to control beavers is to allow an experienced trapper to catch them all during the legal season. Most if not all complaints for beaver removal occur in early summer when beavers are at their most active, remodeling their dams to catch spring runoff and enlarge their ponds, so legal trapping is usually not an option. The next option is to send the conservation officer out to solve the problem. 'Back in the day' the fatigue uniform was unheard of, and the CO would tramp out into the muddy forest, wearing hip boots over the dress uniform to assess the situation. Live trapping and moving the beavers was usually the first attempt made to remove the beavers.

It should be said that live trapping was merely a pipe dream, and was never effective. As soon as the first beaver was caught in the live trap, all the remaining beavers became 'trap smart'. And refused to step into the trap.

The live trap was nothing more than a clam like device covered with chain link fence. When opened and set, the trap would lay flat with the trigger standing up in the middle of the tap. The theory was that the officer would break an opening in the dam, causing a leak. The open live trap would be placed in the open escaping stream. When the beavers heard the rushing water they would come to repair the leak and save the level of the pond. Stepping up onto the trap to assess the situation, the beaver would bump the trigger and be captured with the slamming of the trap around his furry, but surprised little body.

Having given numerous presentations to schools and civic groups that included mention of the ingenuity of beavers, one would think that someone of my intelligence would realize that a beaver would be smarter than to just swim up and step onto a foreign object like a live trap. Well, the beavers were indeed that smart, and I was not. If an animal was in fact caught, it was usually a small yearling, not yet wise to the sneaky ways of game wardens. It was also the only one caught, and probably the subject of copious ridicule by all the other beavers. That one yearling would be transported to another dam out in the wilderness and the trap reset on the problem dam. During my career, live trapping was only attempted twice.

My first experience with the live trap began successfully with the capture of a yearling pup. After he was taken to a new home in the Big Brook marsh just upstream from Hayward Lake I returned to the dam and reset the trap, smug in the belief that the next morning would yield yet another beaver.

Arriving at the dam I found the leak quite effectively repaired, with no sign of the live trap. Now this was a real puzzle. Where was the trap? It was enough to make one talk to oneself.

"Well Wayne, who took your trap?" I asked myself. "Who would *want* to take your trap? Probably some animal rights activist, hey?"

My eye caught the glint of shiny metal approximately four feet down in the newly placed sticks and mud of the repair. There, hopelessly intertwined in the twigs, branches and debris was the live trap! There I was, outsmarted by stubby, grubby little varmints with brains the size of walnuts. Well, maybe we're on level ground when it comes to brains. Nothing to do but spend several hours pulling the dam back apart. How do they weave those branches in there like that? Wish I were being paid by the hour.

The next option was always to attempt to discourage the beavers by blowing their dam apart with explosives. This too, was a pipe dream. Discouraging a beaver is on the same order as trying to insult a moose. You just can't do it. With each act of destruction an active colony of beavers would merely set about cheerfully hauling branches, rocks and mud to rebuild the damaged wall. And with each attempt to thwart their activity, about all I had to show was that I was a few hours closer to retirement, and that much muddier.

The explosives we used were known as kinetics. Composed of ammonium nitrate mixed with a catalyst it was safer than dynamite to transport and use. Set off by an electrical blasting cap and a length of detonation cord, the chemicals came in plastic tubes that could be taped to a wooden stake, one atop the other to make up the appropriate sized charge for the job. Usually two stakes with two sticks of kinetics each, placed six feet or so apart in the mud on the upstream side of the dam was enough to do the job.

As a new CO my instruction in the use of kinetics came in the form of watching the neighboring officer from the next county to the north. No formal training was given, but with the neighboring officer still alive it had to be assumed that he knew what he was doing. It must be admitted that blowing holes in beaver dams was truly fun. Each new complaint presented another challenge as to just how the demolition would be engineered.

When using explosives, the rule of thumb is generally "Use lots". If that doesn't do the trick, the second rule of thumb is "Use lots more". However when it came to blowing beaver dams idea was to use as few sticks of kinetics as possible, using the force of the explosion to loosen the dam and allowing the pressure of the escaping water to push the debris outward and downstream. Sometimes the dam would be several years old with most of the debris on the bottom in a rotted condition, making for a fragile foundation that would easily blow apart.

In those cases one had to be careful of flying rocks and pieces of wood. It was wise to hide behind trees or some other large object when blowing the dams, and a close watch was kept for flying debris. If a rock or branch appeared to be moving to the side it was usually safe. Objects in the air that appeared to be sitting still were to be feared and dodged, as they would be flying directly toward the officer.

Sometimes after several acts of destruction the beavers would give up and move to a less noisy location. Other times more tenacious beavers just kept rebuilding the dam, on into the winter when they could be trapped by a sportsman. One particular dam on North Fox road kept CO's occupied for several generations. During my second summer in Menominee County I received a report that beavers had once again built a dam on North Fox road. A quick look at the dam revealed a concave wall built approximately fifty feet out from the culvert in the road. The dam was quite small although it held back some twenty acres of water about six feet in depth. The dam was easily dismantled by hand and I believed that the pair of newly arrived beavers would soon be on their way to more friendly environs.

Within a week I received a report that the dam on North Fox road was once again in place. This time the dam completely plugged the culvert, as if to say "Here, let's see you take *this one* apart!" After several muddy hours the culvert was cleared and a fence constructed with the help of several Fire Officers. This gave some relief until the pests could be legally trapped.

The last (and I *do* mean last!) time I blew a beaver dam was on Big Brook, just downstream from the Wery road bridge. A local farmer had requested that I do him a favor and knock out the dam that had been flooding his lower field for several years. I should have picked up on the 'several years' part, which could have spoken for the fragility of the dam that held back approximately forty acres of water at a depth of seven feet. The beavers had departed for lack of food, but the dam remained. Normally the removal of this dam should have been a simple matter, and I merely put several sticks of mixed kinetics in my personal car along with a blasting cap, the wire, and my flashlight. I would just knock the dam out on my way to conduct some day-off personal business in town.

The walk from the road down to the dam was easy, but I soon learned that very few trees remained behind which to hide. No problem. There stood an old, dead elm tree a hundred feet downstream from the dam. I would just set a small charge to loosen the dam, hide behind this dead tree, and step deftly out of the way as the debris began to move out and the water began to flow. After setting the charge of two single sticks six feet apart I stepped behind the bole of the dead elm and unscrewed the end of my flashlight to access the battery. Touching the detonation wires to the battery contacts I heard what should have been a dull 'whump' of the kinetics loosening a hole in the dam. Instead I heard the loud 'BAM!', and then the instantaneous 'Wham!' of mud and sticks slamming into the elm tree behind which I stood. The fragile dam had disintegrated with the impact of the blast, rocketing debris and mud downstream at lightning speed. Nor did the impounded water come gently tumbling through the six foot opening in the dam. A huge section of the dam had collapsed and the water was upon me in an instant, waist deep and leaving me clinging to the tree trunk to avoid being washed downstream with the flood.

After nearly half an hour the waters subsided somewhat, allowing me to wade ashore. I was soaked through and covered with mud. The business in town would have to wait; it was time for a nice long warm up in the sauna. Soon I would be moving downstate to Rogers City where I would serve as the commercial fish patrol officer for Lake Huron. Hopefully there would be no need for the use of kinetics on the Great Lakes.

Stacking the good alongside the bad, it must be agreed that the North American Beaver is a truly remarkable animal. On one level I can identify with the beaver. Some of us are made to solve problems. Some of us are made to create problems. But as one old friend once said to me while looking me right in the eye, "Some of y'all, God made just for fun!"

Needy Greedy Dirt Bags

"**S**o what did you do on your day off?" Nate's question caused me to chuckle. I had agreed to take VCO Nate on patrol tonight, more than anything to give him a night out of the house. The late December antlerless season was open for another week, but Nate had hunted long enough and bagged sufficient venison to last the winter. Now he was bored and once again ready to play grownup Cops and Robbers. With his type "A" personality he would have made a good Conservation Officer. After two weeks of missing his homespun wordsmithing, I was happy to have him back in the car.

"Did you really think I'd be able to make it through a day without having to do at least *some* game warden work?" I asked. In fact, today was scheduled for a pass day, but as usual that plan didn't work out. I did, indeed, have a story for Nate.

Reaching into my snack bag Nate pilfered a cookie and took a generous bite, looking instantly startled. "Man! I never tasted anything like *this* before. What kind of cookie is this?"

Kathy had baked chocolate chip cookies that afternoon.

Upon discovering an insufficient amount of chocolate chips, she had merely supplemented the recipe with butterscotch chips, making an approximate fifty-fifty mix of the two. The resulting cookies were surprisingly chewy and delicious. But with Nate's question, I realized that this new type of cookie should have a name.

Noticing a highway sign I said "Those are M-35 cookies."

"They taste great. Make sure to have Kathy give my wife the recipe." That sounded good to me. We'd get twice as many cookies if Laura baked them as well.

"So now tell me what went on today," said Nate. "It takes a lot to get you away from that workshop on your day off."

"Well old friend, it sorta went down like this....."

My son, Shawn and I had been lifting weights at Big Ben's house east of Daggett. Living alone, Ben had converted his living room into a small gym with free weights and resistance workout machines. Throughout the winter Ben and I had been working hard, training for the World Police Olympics to be held in Colorado the next summer.

A late afternoon sun made long shadows on the snow covered fields as we departed for home. A new dusting of snow made a crunching sound under the truck tires as we turned onto the highway. Driving half a mile east I took a side road to the south. This two mile stretch of gravel was a popular road for hunters attempting to get their deer the easy way; by shooting from their vehicles. Small farm fields and scattered forest plots made for good road hunting as the deer gathered to graze in the openings near the road.

Topping a short hill I could see two vehicles in the distance. A light blue pickup truck slowly rolled northward in our direction while a second sedan appeared to be stopped mid lane a half mile to the south, facing us. Shawn and I often played "who's the guilty party" at times like this, discussing the possible activities of those around us.

"I think the slow roller coming our way has a gun," I said.

"He's looking for a nice fat doe to pop from the window of the truck."

"Nope," said Shawn. "He's just a wood cutter on his way home. That car way down there is the road hunter, and I bet he's stopped because he's going to shoot from the car right now."

Shawn's wood cutter determination proved correct, as evidenced by the pile of fire wood in the bed of the passing pickup. "I'll still bet he has a gun," I mumbled.

At first our parked car appeared to be nothing more than a breakdown waiting to be retrieved and repaired. Approaching the old gray sedan, I immediately noticed that the driver's window was rolled down and that the car was unoccupied. Walking around the vehicle I was unable to detect any signs that the driver had been hunting. No gun case, or other hunting equipment could be seen.

As I began walking the snow covered shoulder of the road, looking for foot prints, a sudden "Pow!" came from the cedar swamp, down the ditch bank to the west. Apparently we did indeed have a hunter. Shawn had been right, and would be gloating over this for some time.

Within several minutes a figure approached through the foliage, dragging a small deer. Topping the ditch bank moments later Ronnie Cunith came face to face with the local Game Warden.

Ronnie lived in the shadows of society, keeping a low profile as much as possible. Living from short term jobs, to periods of unemployment compensation, and back to temporary work, Ronnie lived a simple life, augmented by the fruits of opportunistic crime. He was known to have burglarized a number of hunting camps and to poach a variety of fish and game, as evidenced by his criminal record. Throughout the years Ronnie and I had forged a somewhat cautious friendship, cordial in our dealings, but neither ever fully trusting the other.

Startled by our sudden confrontation, Ronnie dropped his lever action 30-30 rifle in the snow and released the foot of the yearling deer, allowing it to slide back down the bank, coming to rest at the foot of one of the many cedars.

"Here Ronnie," I said, picking up the rifle. "Let me unload this and we'll talk this over. Do you know whose land you're on?"

"Homer Jones?" Ronnie asked.

"No, you're a quarter mile south of his line. Those signs on the trees tell us that you're trespassing. Where is your hunter orange jacket or cap?"

"I forgot it. Sorry. I guess I forgot my deer license too."

"Don't you remember, Ronnie? You lost your hunting privileges a year ago when I caught you shining. You can't hunt for another year," I said. "Why didn't you have your gun in a case? You know it's illegal to transport an uncased firearm."

Ronnie hung his head. "Jeez, I just forgot. Listen, I'm really sorry about this. I had to get something to eat. Can you give me any kind of a break?"

"Well, let me get back into the truck and write some of this down, and see how this all shakes out."

Ronnie stood by the side of my pickup as I retrieved my ticket book from the glove box. While police officers of other agencies usually enforce the law only when in uniform and working a designated shift, Conservation Officers often carry police equipment while off duty and make a number of arrests in plain clothes.

Sometimes when interviewing a suspect an officer will mention something about the case that he may suspect, but does not know for a fact, to see what his bluff might produce. "Ronnie, when you shot this deer, why couldn't you have at least gotten out of the car?" I asked.

Of course I hadn't witnessed the initial shooting, but Ronnie was unaware of that bit of information, as evidenced by his nearly explosive reaction. Shawn sat in the passenger seat, making choking sounds as he attempted to hide his laughter.

"Jeepers Crumps!" cried Ronnie using typical U P expletives. "Ain't there *anything* you don't know!? Where were ya hiding? Ya *had* to see me shoot!"

"Well now Ronnie, you know I can't give away my secrets," I said. "Let's see what we have here. We have trespassing, no hunter orange, hunting with privileges revoked, uncased firearm in a motor vehicle, loaded firearm in a motor vehicle, untagged deer, hunt from a motor vehicle, illegal killing of whitetail deer, to name a few. Of course I won't charge you with all of them because many of them overlap, but that's the menu we have to pick from."

Ronnie looked as nervous as a pig stuck under a gate. "Well, ya got me dead to rights. What are you gonna do?"

"How about you take a ticket for discharging a firearm adjacent to private property. That will keep the hunting and the deer out of it. I'm going to take the serial number of your rifle down and have you sign the ticket, proving that you had the gun here at the scene. I'll return the gun to you right now so you can dry out the snow and clean it. Now I'm going to head for home and I won't be back. If that deer is still here in the morning, somebody is going to get a ticket for littering," I said.

Accepting the citation, Ronnie was shaking with relief. "Man, I thought you'd be taking me to jail," he said as he opened the trunk of his car and set the rifle inside. Giving a big smile and a salute he was on his way north, more than likely to pick up the deer once he was sure that I was not going to return.

On the ride home Shawn laughed the whole way. "Wow, was I right, or what! Old Ronnie was right up to his eyeballs in violations. Why did you let him off so easy?"

"Nothing is ever easy with Ronnie anymore," I said. "When the magistrate gets this citation she will sock him as a repeat offender; maximum fines all the way. It won't do a whole lot of good to 'double dip' him. Citing him for the deer would merely give him some jail time, and fines that he can't pay. We're feeding him on either side of the bars."

"Well it just about killed me to keep from laughing the whole time. And *I* called it!" bragged Shawn.

"So that's what happened on my day off," I said to Nate as we pulled into the parking lot at the Scott Paper Dam. The story had lasted the whole trip to Menominee and now it was time to hide and watch for late season Salmon snaggers at the fishing site on the Menominee River.

"Needy, Greedy Dirt Bags," said Nate as we gathered our flashlights and binoculars.

"What kind of gibberish are you talking now," I asked, unable to attach anything Nate had just said with anything logical. Nate often said things that made no sense; just keeping up his end of the conversation.

"Needy Greedy Dirt Bags. I heard it on the radio when I came home from work today. I didn't catch what it was about," answered Nate. "But it kind of describes a lot of the people we have to deal with."

"No, I'm sure it's something that made sense, and you heard it wrong. But as usual your Natley-ism is more accurate. It does seem to describe a certain faction of our society."

Nate gave his signature 'Pussum-eatin' grin. "Yeah, c'mon. Let's go get some more!"

Champions Among Us

Along the east side of Menominee County there runs a stream known as the Big Cedar River. Her peaceful waters provide recreation for fishermen, boaters and swimmers from Hermansville at the headwaters for some fifty miles to the south where she rolls into Green Bay at the town of Cedar River. The usually placid depths give the lie to the wild, bawdy, freewheeling past of the logging era when small dams backed up acres of spring runoff water to be released for the floating of millions of board feet of White Pine and hardwood to the many local lumber mills. More than one logger lost his life to her raging flows; pulled under by rogue currents or crushed by colliding logs. Today the dams are gone and only on rare occasions does the Big Cedar collect enough spring runoff at any one time to become a vestige of the roaring dragon she once used to be. One such occasion was in April of nineteen ninety-one.

The bright afternoon sun had brought the thermometer up to an inspiring forty-five degrees, augmenting the week long thaw that had produced a decent amount of runoff and threatened to overflow many of the local roadside ditches throughout the county. Flood warnings were in effect along the Menominee River south of Wallace as they were every spring when the river ice broke free and backed up in the flood plains.

The beeping of the Cedarville Township fire department pager at 2:45 PM destroyed my plans of coaching track at Stephenson High School, calling me to the fire hall for a water rescue. No details other than "boater in distress" were given, along with the address of Lyn Peterson, a resident on the Big Cedar approximately seven miles north on highway 551.

The Peterson residence is a beautiful, large log home on the Big Cedar River nearly a mile west of the county road through old growth stands of Cedars and Hemlocks. Upon arrival at the lodge our crew was unable to locate any one on the east side of the river. On the west side of the stream were several people, all of which appeared soaking wet and chilled to the bone, waving and shouting for us to come around by road and pick them up on the other side.

The story which was later related to us was one of true heroism, or should I say heroine-ism. It seems that two local residents of Cedar River, Will and Scotty, had decided to canoe the Big Cedar River from the Red Bridge down to the village that afternoon. Their decision to conduct the voyage while the water was high did not take into account that at high levels the river is at its most dangerous. Tree branches that are normally several feet above the water become "Sweepers" just inches below the surface and normally harmless small eddies become deadly whirlpools, reminiscent of historic days gone by. Couple this set of circumstances with the fact that our two canoeists were somewhat in debt when it came to common sense, and we had the perfect recipe for disaster.

Having only one life preserver between the pair, Scotty had opted to tie the bow rope around his ankle under the mistaken idea that should the canoe capsize, he would remain in contact with the canoe, which should float. Will, in the aft of the canoe had donned the only wearable life jacket possessed by the pair.

All went well until the canoe rounded the bend above the old logging dam across from the Peterson cabin. As the canoe turned sideways in the current, Will grabbed an overhanging branch in an effort to prevent the canoe from spinning around. With the canoe held stationary above the water, the craft slid sideways, capsizing and bending double around the old dam foundation. Will drifted free of the canoe and swam to shore on the west bank. Scotty shot downstream until he came to the end of the bow rope and there hung feet first in the current, unable to reach his ankle and undo the rope.

Hearing cries for help, Lyn looked out the front door of the lodge to see Scotty bobbing in the current at the end of the rope. The current spun him like a fishing lure as he fought desperately to regain the surface for a breath of air. Only able to inhale a small gulp of air every thirty seconds or so, it would not be long before Scotty would succumb to fatigue, stop surfacing and drown.

Resisting the urge to immediately run out and assist, Lyn picked up the phone and dialed 911, giving her location and the nature of the emergency to the dispatcher. Running to her own canoe Lyn entered the river a short distance upstream and ferried across the raging current, gaining the opposite shore and shouting for Will to pull her canoe out of the river. Entering the icy waters she jumped out to grasp the bow rope, fought the current until she reached Scotty, and untied the rope which held his foot. Scotty shot down the sluice and out into the main current to be rescued and taken to shore by Lyn.

By the time our fire crew reached the location of the trio they were in the early stages of hypothermia. Blankets were distributed and we returned to the Peterson cabin where hot chocolate and coffee warmed the survivors who were given a ride back to the town of Cedar River. Lyn accepted our congratulations and thanks, but refused offers to be interviewed by the local newspaper for her act of courage.

Another incident which could have ended very badly if not for the quick response of one courageous off duty policeman happened in nineteen seventy-eight, give or take a year or two.

One evening during the Pike runs I stopped at the Menominee county Jail for a cup of their sludge so loosely referred to as coffee. Rex the dispatcher greeted me with more than his usual zesty good humor.

"Wow Rex, you seem to be in a really good mood tonight. What's up?"

"I just got a hug and a kiss from a really beautiful woman," said Rex. "Only saw her once before in my life."

"Okay, now this sounds too good," I said. "You have to give me the story."

"Well it starts quite a few years ago," began Rex. "I was fly fishing on the Big Cedar River, in the rapids just below the DNR camp ground."

It was a hot June morning and the sun beat down on the fast moving water, making Polaroid sun glasses a necessity. The river was approximately seventy-five feet wide and running fast, waist deep in the center of the crystal clear current. Large polished rocks hid a number of good sized Rainbow Trout, the target of Rex's fly fishing efforts.

Casting upstream, Rex drifted his dry fly through the current repeatedly. Suddenly amid the roiling foam at the center of the current, a small face appeared as the fly drifted by.

More from reflex than conscious action Rex threw his fly rod towards shore and entered the current, concentrating on the spot where he had last seen the face. In the middle of the stream the current threatened to sweep him off his feet as he desperately scanned the rapids. Seeing nothing he began to lurch downstream trying to locate something; anything that would make some sense of what he thought he had just witnessed.

Then, a flash of white. A diaper! Then, a baby drifting swiftly down through the current. Thrashing, fighting to keep his feet in the deep water, Rex caught the small floating body, grasping one leg in a death grip.

At the foot of the rapids Rex waded to shore, the small body cradled in his arms. The child was a toddler, probably no more than eight months old, and she wasn't breathing. Her ashen white color was rapidly turning a shade of bluish-gray. Turning the little girl on her stomach in one hand Rex administered several sound slaps to her back. The body convulsed, choked and began to breathe.

"My baby! My baby! You've got my baby! Give her to me!"

Rex heard the distraught woman before he saw her. Running down to the shore she reached for the toddler with one hand, pushing against Rex's face with the other, shouting at Rex as if he were a kidnapper.

"Hold it Lady! Let's see if we can figure this out," said Rex, trying to calm the panicked woman.

"I'll call the police!" shouted the woman

"I AM the police," said Rex. "Now just where did you leave your baby in the first place."

"I didn't leave her anywhere. She was with my husband."

A short walk upstream solved the mystery. There in a lawn chair was the father; asleep, or perhaps more likely passed out, with two empty beer bottles on the ground beside the chair. The woman took the baby without as much as a thank you to Rex. Rex left his name with the negligent couple and their fortunate daughter.

Fast forward to the spring evening with me enjoying a cup of mud with Rex at the jail.

"Tonight as I came in for work I stopped at the bowling alley for a burger. I was enjoying my supper when this gorgeous young lady taps me on the shoulder and asks if I'm Rex Zelinski. I no sooner say 'yes' than she gives me a bear hug and plants a lip lock on me that took my breath away. My head was still spinning when she says 'You saved my life. Pulled me out of the Cedar River twenty years ago.' I'm going to be savoring this for a long time to come!"

Menominee County has many heroes such as these. None of them consider themselves as such, just everyday people doing what was required at the time. If Rex recognizes himself in this story he will probably offer me a knuckle sandwich. I do not care. I'm proud to have known and worked with him. Lyn Peterson WILL give me knuckle sandwich if she can catch me. I think I can still outrun her.

So Kudos to both of you, Rex and Lyn. Though you both deserve medals of valor you refuse to consider yourselves anything more than just two average people. Two people who were able to snatch two living souls from the jaws of the Big Cedar River.

By the Book

My first piece of issued equipment upon joining the ranks of the Michigan Conservation Officers was a Law Book. This compact paperback edition of some three hundred pages described every iniquity a person could commit against our natural resources, be it polluting the air, land or water; depleting the stocks of fish or game; defiling the concept of fair chase; recreating in an unsafe manner; stealing the collateral property of the state such as minerals or timber; or any other of a motley assortment of sins a person could perpetrate that might raise the ire of the good people of the State.

A larger volume composed of a three ring binder with removable pages was issued for use in the home office of the CO. We were told that as changes in the laws came about, we were to remove the old version of the particular law and replace it with the new amended document. WHAT?! Wait a minute. I thought "The law" was "The Law", plain and simple. What could possibly come along that would require the law to be changed? I was to learn over the years that "The law" was a fluid, living thing, changing constantly as new recreational vehicles and devices were invented, new species of fish and game were introduced, new safety rules became necessary and the changing of the times reformed our concepts of recreation and conservation.

Some of the old laws became archaic, no longer applicable and no longer enforced. The law which made it illegal to possess venison longer than ninety days beyond the close of deer season became impractical with the advent of home freezers, but the law remained on the books. Numerous such outdated rules still remain on the books, there having been no good reason to eliminate them. Occasionally they are used in instances when other laws might not accurately apply.

Occasionally an officer may tend to follow the rules more closely than is comfortable for the citizenry he serves. The officer who writes a speeding ticket for one mile per hour over the limit or the CO who arrests a fisherman in possession of a fish a sixteenth of an inch too short are said to go "Right by the book", and their enforcement efforts are not appreciated. To say that an officer goes "Right by the book" is usually an insult, insinuating that he is too officious to serve the proper intent of the law. Yet there are instances when closely following the letter of the law is exactly what the customer wants, or at least seems to at the moment.

An early snow had fallen on the Chalk Hills forest, west of the village of Banat, and the deer hunters were happy. The inch of soft whiteness made the deer easy to see and track. The wet snow was silent under the boots, increasing the chances of bagging a trophy buck. It was also an ideal day to be a Game Warden. Reading sign and tracking are as important to the CO as it is to the hunter and today's snowfall made the job far more enjoyable.

The state owned property in this area was peppered with small privately owned parcels of land used for hunting, and in this area it was common for landowners to construct illegal permanent deer blinds in the state forest adjacent to their property. Walking the logging trails, looking for tracks in the snow was the easiest and least intrusive method of finding these blinds and enforcing the law. On this beautiful sunny morning, I was good with that.

I had been hiking west under a canopy of leafless mature hardwoods on a two track road, half a mile from the patrol car when my eye caught a spot of blaze orange through the swamp two hundred yards to the south. Backing up I saw it again; a hunter up in a tree stand. Time to mosey over and determine if he's an archery hunter or an illegal rifle hunter. The tree stand would have to be portable since this location was several hundred yards from private property.

A small stream flowed across my course of travel as I picked my way through a thick carpet of moss under low hanging cedar boughs. Stepping gingerly on a rotted log to cross the creek I startled a decent sized brook trout that shot upstream to hide under another log. I'd have to remember this next summer and take my son fishing here. Presently I walked up onto higher ground to the tree where the hunter sat.

A single set of three wheeler tracks emerged from the swamp to the south, circled the tree and returned to the swamp. A single set of foot prints traversed the distance from the three wheeler tracks to the base of the tree where the hunter had climbed up into the blind using footholds screwed into the tree trunk. Someone had ferried the hunter out to the blind on the ORV and probably returned to their own hunting blind in the private land.

The hunter was a fourteen year old boy. While he was legally in possession of a hunting license and dressed in the required blaze orange hunting gear, he was hunting from a permanent blind on state property, hunting from a raised platform with a rifle, and hunting without adult supervision as required by law. I advised the young hunter of these violations, asking the whereabouts of the person who had left him here. The lad said that his father was in his blind about a quarter mile to the south. We set off to find the father.

A hundred feet or so into the private land I heard, rather than saw the father. "Get out of here! You're on private land!" was the greeting shouted from the ground blind; a squat plywood box covered with evergreen boughs.

Off to the right of the blind, down at the end of a brushed out shooting lane a pile of cabbages, pumpkins, and corn was visible, along with the customary block of mineral salt. Approaching the blind I recognized the angry face of Walter Sutherland. Walter lived in Illinois, but spent much of his time here at his hunting camp. He was known to have a mean temper and very little respect for authority. Again he shouted "You're trespassing, get off my property!"

"I'll be glad to Wally, as soon as we finish the business at hand," I began.

"That's MR. Sutherland to you," Walter interjected.

"Whatever, sir. I need to know why your son is hunting unsupervised. At his age you have to be with him while hunting," I said.

"Prove it. Prove that he didn't go out there by himself. All you've got is circumstantial evidence. You didn't see anything. Just try to prove it in court," said Walter.

I decided to spare him the argument about information and belief. "I guess you might be one who wants to go by the book," I said.

"That's correct. Right by the book! You just see if you can use the book, then get off my land."

"Well okay sir, the book says that it is illegal to hunt over salt. You are under arrest for hunting over salt. May I see your identification, please?" I asked.

"What?! They NEVER arrest anyone for that. That's an outdated law. You can't do this!" exclaimed Walter.

"Normally I wouldn't, but you requested, no, you demanded

it. We aim to please. And when the judge sees this violation he's going to order me to give him the particular facts of this unusual citation. That means mentioning one set of tracks to the tree stand, your three wheeler here at the blind, no gun cases for transporting the firearms on the motor vehicle, no helmets for the ORV, your son hunting unsupervised from a permanent tree stand on state land, and last of all that salt block two hundred feet off the end of your gun barrel," I explained.

The summons for hunting over salt was issued to a silent but fuming Mr. Sutherland and he was left to brood over his decision, knowing that on Wednesday he would be facing a very stern but fair judge in District Court. The son was not cited. It was not my policy to arrest juveniles unless it is absolutely necessary.

This was the only instance in which I ever used this old, out dated law. And I am not proud of that particular transaction. Had the circumstances been different I would not have used it then. I'm also certain that in the future my friend Walter will think twice about wanting to go "Right by the book."

Tracking the Greenwoods Turkey(s)

W hile I have never attained the title of Detective, I have always been intrigued by the art of a technique known as 'cold tracking'. This aspect of law enforcement involves taking a small bit of evidence and developing it into a case that results in the successful prosecution of a guilty party.

Often a poacher, having committed a violation, will carefully remove or destroy as much evidence of the crime as possible to escape detection. This may involve carrying rather than dragging a poached animal, wiping up blood spatters, picking up spent shell casings, or burying unused body parts of illegally taken animals. On occasion some small detail would be overlooked. It might be an envelope dropped from a poacher's car, or perhaps the imprint of a license plate number in a snowbank left by the violator as he backed around to leave the scene. Litterbugs were often caught using the lot numbers printed on the bottoms of beer cans, compared with those still in possession of the guilty party. On one occasion it was the hide of a deer, unique in its partial albino markings compared with numerous photos taken by an entire neighborhood of hobbyist wildlife feeders that provided the evidence necessary to build a solid case.

I once knew a homicide detective who used to say "My day begins when yours ends." Thus it was with cold tracking. Once the crime has been committed and the dust settles; then the fun began. Fun for me. Was it fun for the poacher, who often felt the hand at the end of the long arm of the law, slowly tightening its grip? I guess I didn't really care. The crowning moment always came at the conclusion of the investigation when the miscreant was presented with a citation for his 'perfect crime' from which he thought he had escaped free and clear.

I have never been one to delight in the punishment of those who broke the law. I have always felt that if law enforcement could be as simple as merely catching the law breaker and not have the offense repeated, I would happily consider my job well done. That being said I must admit that a certain amount of satisfaction was enjoyed when a bad guy was brought to justice. Then it was time to move on to the next project. No concern was given to the degree of penalties meted out to convicted individuals. It was enough to know that I had served the people of the state.

Cold tracking is not for the faint of heart, nor the strictly honest. To catch a thief it sometimes takes a thief, and one may have to practice a certain degree of deception. If you're going to catch bad guys you may have to associate with some very bad people, pretending to be someone you're not; giving information that isn't completely true. The case of the Greenwoods turkey(s) is an example of three otherwise pretty good sportsmen who allowed their excitement to overpower their respect for the law. A little cold tracking resulted in their being apprehended, much to the satisfaction of one land owner.

The call came as I walked through the front door, anticipating a tasty supper. Omer Granville sounded angry and agitated.

"Wayne, this is Omer from Greenwoods. I just chased some trespassers off my property. They made off with a wild turkey from under the apple trees in my yard!"

"I thought you lived at the end of a long driveway," I said. "Don't you have that sawmill a quarter mile in from the road?"

"That's right," Said Omer. "I was watching TV about four o'clock when I heard shots right out in my front yard. These three guys had come in all the way from the road. They grabbed a wild turkey and took off running. There's no way they could have missed all my 'Keep out' signs out there along the road. I jumped in my truck and headed for the highway. By the time I got to the road they were getting into a pickup truck and took off at a high rate of speed. I got the license plate number here for you if you want it."

"Good work Omer," I said. "I might be able to track at least one of them down with the plate number."

A week later on a Monday afternoon I sat down at the desk of the district biology tech in Stephenson. The license plate number given by Mr. Granville had given me the name and address of the pickup owner. Hopefully this information would identify at least one of the three trespassers. If I could convincingly sound like a curious biologist I might be able to do some good.

Calling the information line I obtained the telephone number of the truck owner and dialed the number in the downstate town of Novi. Dick Bowerman answered on the fourth ring.

"Hi Mr. Bowerman," I began. "This is Wayne with the DNR. We're just tying up some end of season things here, and I was wondering how you did up here with your turkey hunt."

"Oh, I didn't get a turkey," said Dick. "My buddy Tom got a nice gobbler, though."

"Let's see, Tom....Hey, what would his last name be?" I asked.

"It's Tom Lapan," said Dick.

"Hmmmm, I don't see him on our list of successful appli-
cants," I said. "Would you happen to have his name and address;
maybe his telephone number, and I can get the rest of the information from him?"

"Sure!" said Dick. The address and phone number for Mr.
Lapan were given and I thanked Mr. Bowerman. I then dialed
up Tom.

"Tom! Glad I got ahold of you!" I said. "This is Wayne with
the DNR here in Stephenson. I was just finalizing some things
and I wanted to know how you did with this season's turkey
hunt."

"Oh hey, I got a real nice gobbler," said Tom. "Twenty one
pounds."

"Say now, that's one really nice turkey," I said. "It's not every
day a guy has that kind of luck. Did you call him in yourself?"

"No, actually my two buddies helped me," said Tom.

"Let's see if I have cards for them," I said. "What are their
names?"

"That would be Larry Stock and Dick Bowerman," said
Tom.

"Okay let's see here.....I have a Dick Bowerman in Novi,
and a Larry Stock without an address or phone number.
Would you happen to have Larry's information?"

Tom happily supplied Larry's address and telephone number. A call to Larry verified that he had, indeed been hunting
in Menominee County with Dick and Tom. While a certain
amount of deceit (Yeah, okay, a LOT of deceit) was used to
get the required information, it must be realized that none of
the trio would have co-operated in any way had I been straight
forward in my investigation, and the trespassers would have
gone free. The names and addresses served to search up dates
of birth and citations were written for recreational trespass. A
Conservation who lived in the same county as the guilty trio
received and served the trespassing citations. Dismay and anger were expressed by all three guilty hunters. Their fines

were promptly paid by mail. To their grousing about all the deception perpetrated by myself, the arresting officer replied, "Yeah, almost as bad as shooting a turkey from someone's front yard and refusing to stop and talk with the landowner."

Through the years many cases were solved by cold tracking. Not all were successful, but occasionally when the right events came together and the violators were brought to answer for their crimes it was all worthwhile. Many examples could be related here. But those, good and faithful reader, are other stories.

Those Sacred Cars

A ny time someone ventures into a new field of endeavor
it becomes immediately apparent that one must know
what the new boss, or administration considers important. In my case one might think that officer safety, public
relations or working knowledge of the law would take the fore-
front concerning aspects of the job upon which the new officer
should concentrate. Well, get ready for a surprise. If you're a
new conservation officer, the name of the game is your vehicle,
and how to keep it in pristine, showroom condition. I was to
learn this the hard way; by trial and error. Mostly error.

Don't get me wrong. I have never been a daredevil driver. I
just happened to be assigned a county wherein the deer population was above average, and it was necessary to work during
those hours when the deer were out in force, available to those
who would take them illegally. Somehow this information was
never relayed to the Department of Management and Budget
who supplied our patrol cars. For some reason car/animal collisions sent them into a tailspin from which letters of reprimand
issued like brass casings from a machine gun.

I'm sure it was easy to look from the windows of the Lansing office, watching the careful drivers negotiating the lanes and spaces of the parking lots below and think "How can that CO in the U P be so careless? He must be just batting down those night time side roads at eighty miles an hour without lights, hitting anything and everything in his way." Curiously I have never hit anything, be it deer or other vehicles while driving without lights. It's when the lights are on and animals are confused and blinded that collisions occur.

For a time during my tenure in the Upper Peninsula we were subjected to something during our monthly district meetings known as "The monthly report". Conservation officers throughout the district would meet at the District Office and the District Supervisor would relate the previous month's activities which would include various programs conducted by the officers, number of arrests made, and of course, vehicle accidents. At most of these meetings I could be counted on to "make the print".

"Wayne Coleman had an accident" the report would read in accusation. Some State Senator had decreed that any and all accidents incurred by police officers would go on the officer's personal driving record. It did not matter that the fender bender was the result of a parking lot dent or an officer putting his vehicle in the path of a runaway car to save lives, the report came back the same. This officer had an accident, and it was going on his personal driving record.

My nemeses were deer that constantly defied natural law and attempted to occupy the same place at the same time as my patrol car. It didn't matter how I played it. One time while driving at forty miles per hour enroute to a shining complaint an eight point buck jumped over the hood of the patrol car and crashed through the windshield, penetrating my left hand with a scatter shot of glass shards and putting my partner under the dashboard in a heap. "Wayne Coleman had an accident". Once on a side road during deer season I found myself in the middle of a deer drive which sent a group of six deer around both ends of my patrol car. One brave buck jumped over the top of the car, clicking his hoofs on the roof, causing dents and scratches in the paint. "Wayne Coleman had an accident". One night I stopped to allow several deer to run across in front of the car. One yearling was a bit slow to get the message and ran into the left rear quarter panel of the parked car, causing a dent and flaking of paint. "Wayne Coleman had an accident".

On other occasions I could understand Lansing's reasoning and need for a report. One night I was working with our under cover van, trying to capture a poaching ring suspected of working in our county. The first snowfall of the year had made highway U S 41 slippery and drivers were not yet accustomed to winter driving. Slowing to make a left hand turn onto Belgiumtown road I was struck in the rear by a driver who was not prepared to stop. Making the turn I pulled to the side of the road, followed by the offending vehicle. Upon seeing my uniform the driver uttered those most famous two words, the first of which was "Oh..." The damage was not serious enough to require the presence of another officer of the law and I took a hasty accident report, attributing the collision to road conditions and sent the driver on his way. No damage could be seen on his vehicle, but of course there was damage to the van I was driving. "Wayne Coleman had an accident".

On another occasion we were working in an attempt to catch the same poaching ring when I was called to intercept a deer shiner headed towards the village of Daggett. At three o'clock in the morning the road was devoid of all traffic and travel to the area at high speed was relatively safe. Coming up on the curve north of Daggett at seventy miles an hour my eye caught a brown blur to my left. The immediate sickening "Bang!" and the splash of blood and manure on the windshield told me that my patrol for the night was all done.

Pulling to the shoulder and assessing the damage I could

see that the grille, the radiator and the deer had become one, and everything that could possibly be damaged had indeed been destroyed. Headlights, cowling, fenders and hood would have to be replaced along with many parts under the hood. But glory of glories, the engine was still running.

At that moment the radio from the airplane overhead sprang to life, informing me that our deer shiner was not on the highway, but was coming in on Dog Town road, half a mile to the east. Figuring that I had a gallon of anti-freeze left in the engine I cut the squalling serpentine belt with my jack knife, freeing the engine to run as well as it could, and roared off to Dog Town, sprinkling incidental parts as I went.

The overheated engine was cackling like an angry Guinea Hen as I pulled up on Main Street in Dog Town, making a head-on stop on the shiner in the center of the village. The occupants of the pickup had no weapons with which to kill a deer and appeared to be out on a late night joy ride, just looking at the wild life. It was determined that one citation would be issued for shining after eleven P M. Finishing the paperwork I returned to my demolished patrol car to await the arrival of the wrecker and found several Conservation officers who had sped to the scene to offer backup assistance. All the guys were snickering and laughing.

The chief undercover officer approached and slapped me on the shoulder. "If this ain't the most typical 'Wayne Coleman' scene you can imagine. Your car is demolished, steaming and clattering in a state of near total destruction, and you're standing there, foot up on the bumper, calmly writing out a ticket. Worst of all, you'll have that heap running like a song by tomorrow afternoon!" Be that as it may, the monthly report read "Wayne Coleman had an accident".

Strangely enough, when an accident of significant magnitude occurred, the Lansing office was unusually silent. On one occasion my patrol car was totaled by a freight train. Not one word of this mishap issued from the Ivory Tower. Perhaps the thought that I had suffered enough trauma prompted a reprieve from their normal complaints.

Eventually a learning process evolved and areas of intensely high deer populations would simply be avoided unless travel in that area were absolutely necessary. Deer guards, politely called 'brush guards' were installed on the front of patrol cars. Those simple devices saved many reams of paperwork as numerous impacts were absorbed by the protective angle iron and steel diamond pattern mesh. The guards were extremely durable, to the point that I once hit a deer broadside at seventy miles an hour and was able to continue on to persuade a crazed farm boy not to stab his brother with a butcher knife, but that's another story. After a few years my driving record improved and I was no longer a target of ridicule at the monthly meetings. The bean counters could now focus their worries on more important matters, like all the unnecessary miles we were driving.

Bravery or Cowardice?

One of the most common attributes used to describe police officers is that they are brave. Those serving the public in the capacity of enforcers of the law are often pictured as those upon whom we can depend, whatever the situation. They're occasionally expected to step in and act without fear and carry the day, saving us from all types of violence and tragedy. Matt Dillon would meet the gunfighter on Main Street at high noon, always calm and confident. The bad guy would draw first, but Matt was always faster and deadly accurate. We all just expected that. In truth, as police officers, we would like to picture ourselves as equally brave and valiant. Should it be suggested that we may have acted in less than a courageous manner in a given situation, we take it personally, and do our best to justify our actions to prove that we are not cowards.

During my career there were times when I have experienced fear. Lots of it at times. There were occasions when I had doubts about some of the decisions I have made. That all goes with the territory. The life of a CO is made up of 'forks in the road', and scary things. But the word I never wanted any-one to use when describing me was "Coward". For this reason the events of the night of September 22, 1985 gave me reason to question my courage.

It was one of those warm, foggy early autumn evenings along the Big Cedar River. The aspen trees had started their annual turn from green to gold and the maples were just be-ginning to show a hint of yellow and red. Salmon had appeared in the river the previous week and anglers would soon be making their appearance along the banks, eager to catch the still silver, firm fish. With few fishermen as yet and good fish in the river this was the prime week for a poacher to set an illegal gill net below the rapids, located a mile north of highway M-35 along county road 551.

At ten PM I cached the patrol car a short distance down a two-track trail known to local CO's as the North Pull-off. From the pull-off the mile walk downstream to the rapids gave me a chance to assess conditions along the river. The hem-locks dripped moisture from the mist as I walked the soft forest floor along the riverbank, listening for the splash of Salmon in the riffles. Traffic along 551 was nearly nonexistent and most of the seasonal homes were vacant, making for a nearly silent journey as I patrolled downstream. Walking slowly so as not to work up a sweat I could see the light from one of these houses as I neared the rapids.

The summer home of George Brooks was occupied, with three cars in the driveway. A quartz dusk to dawn light illumi-nated the yard behind the house. During the evening hours at this time of year several deer were often present in this yard as they fed at a small bait pile under the yard light. George main-tained the bait on weekend visits while up from his residence in Chicago where he supposedly worked with one of the many police departments. George's house was located across the road from the river, a stone's throw from the water's edge. A large white steel pole building occupied his yard on the east side of the house. It was rumored that George and his Chicago friends were frequent poachers who snagged and netted Salmon and killed a number of illegal deer each fall, taking their ill-gotten gains back to Chicago.

I had met Mr. Brooks the previous summer as I checked bank fishermen along 551. George was very friendly; too friendly from my point of view, quick to mention his police affiliation and more than eager to brag about his shooting skills. After a short time of listening, I became suspicious that George was merely the member of some sort of police auxiliary, hanging around the station house for whatever benefits his 'wannabee cop' status could gain him. I began to suspect that the various Illinois registered vehicles that often frequented his driveway were unscrupulous friends from the big city, taking advantage of nature's bounty in the form of illegally taken fish and game. All I had to do was prove it.

Shielding the flashlight lens with my hand I carefully checked the river below the rapids for nets. Not able to find any, I resumed my patrol downstream from the Brooks residence when a sudden "Pow!" The neat, whip-like crack of a .22 rifle startled me to high alert. The rifle shot had come from the rear of the Brooks pole building. Moving swiftly, yet as carefully as possible I positioned myself back across the road from the house with a partial view of the back yard. Immediately, two shadowy figures drifted through the heavy mist from the pole building toward the bait pile. The small body of a Whitetail fawn lay near the bait pile beneath the yard light. Each grasping a front leg, the two figures swiftly dragged the small deer back into the pole building. Around the house peered the small face of a neighbor known to me as Dizzy Olsen, watching the road for any approaching vehicles. Dizzy had been the one who had complained about Salmon being illegally netted. It was evident that he was playing both sides of the law; reporting violations and serving as a lookout for the poachers as well. This was not going to bode well for him.

It should be mentioned that my heart was in my throat. A significant violation had been committed right before my eyes and I was experiencing what deer hunters refer to as "Buck fever". My first instinct was to cross the road as soon as Dizzy disappeared back into the pole building, and make the arrests. But something held me back. I couldn't describe it as fear, but my gut feeling was telling me something that I'd never before experienced. "Stay back. Let it go," it said. I felt light headed, confused. I had encountered bigger, meaner people in the past and my practice was always to wade right in and catch the bad guys.

I walked up the road to the patrol car, turning back several times. The Game Warden in me was telling me to go back and confront the poachers, but something else was directing me to the patrol car, away from this experience. I prayed that this something was not cowardice.

The drive home was a long one, with my thoughts going many directions at once. This just wasn't the Wayne Coleman I was used to. I didn't walk away from the bad guys. Maybe I could figure it out in the morning; things often looked better in the light of day. I would try to get some sleep and meet with Sergeant Bart. I had to try to get to the bottom of this.

The bleak, yellow sunrise did not look much better than the sleepless night. Meeting with Sergeant Bart over lunch at the Village Inn, I poured out the events of the night before. Bart listened attentively, nodding; his poker face revealing nothing of his thoughts.

"Now let me get this straight," said Bart at the finish of my report. "You heard the shot and saw two guys drag the deer into the pole building. Dizzy Olsen acted as the crow so they were obviously pretty well organized."

"I guess you could say that," I answered.

"Your patrol car is a mile upstream. Backup help is not an option. By the time you went for the car and got some help the deer would have been quartered and in the freezer. You'd need a search warrant. Lots of luck getting one with that Lilly livered student intern in the prosecutor's office. Thankfully he's leaving soon."

"Okay, but why didn't I confront them right then? Why did I walk away?" I asked, needing some sort of explanation.

"That's how cops disappear and are never found. You knew these guys to probably be big time players. They hadn't committed any felonies last night, but they are more than likely used to solving their problems in a violent manner. Somewhere in that gurgling brew that you refer to as a mind you realized that, and for once in your life you refrained from taking one of those crazy chances I'm always cautioning you about. You did the right thing. Now stop beating yourself up and let's go get those boys." Bart even bought lunch.

George's new cream-colored pickup was the solitary vehicle in the yard as we pulled into his driveway. We were greeted with a hearty "Hello!" as George answered the door and invited us in. "Sit down! I just made some coffee," said George.

Bart and I stayed on our feet, declining the coffee. "George, we have to talk about the deer you and your friends shot last night," began Bart. As George raised his hands and began to speak in protest, Bart waved him off. "To start with, you're in possession of illegal deer, no argument about it. Further, we can search your friends' houses in Chicago and arrest them for violations of the Lacey act, which means transporting illegal fish or game across state lines. Your violation means five days in jail, a thousand dollars in restitution for the deer, and whatever the court wants to assess in fines and costs, as well as revocation of your hunting licenses for four years. Let's have a look at the illegal meat."

George's complexion turned ashen. "What are you talking about? I don't know anything about any illegal deer! You'll need a search warrant to look around here."

"We'll do it any way you want," said Bart. "But if we get a warrant, we're going to take this place apart. You work with cops so we can speak plain English. If you let us look around and we find something illegal, we can talk about a charge a lot less than the illegal deer. If we have to get a warrant, you might as well call your attorney right now, because we're going to do the whole nine yards."

"Well, let me see," said a much deflated George. "I suppose I could let you check the place over. Promise you won't tear everything apart."

George's refrigerator showed nothing other than a few weekend groceries and a six-pack of cheap beer. The pole building was an entirely different matter. The spacious building looked like a tool supply warehouse. Implements from automotive tools to woodworking lathes, planers and saws, to lawn tractors occupied the shop in neatly organized rows. I couldn't help wondering how much of this inventory had been purchased at "special police discount" prices.

Two large chest freezers lined the west wall of the building. One freezer contained what appeared to be frozen beef, commercially packaged, while the other was designated for fish and game. A number of packages of frozen Salmon appeared to have been processed the previous year and were labeled as such. One small package caught our eye. There on top of some older packages labeled "deer meat" lay an unlabeled parcel containing the tenderloins of one small deer, not yet completely frozen.

"I don't know what to tell you about that," George said weakly, "except that I didn't do it."

"Here's the deal George," said Bart. "We have an eye witness that saw the whole thing. He was here when you and the boys in those two other cars shot the deer and dragged it into this building. He is more than happy to testify in court. If we look, we'll find the tarp you used to cover the floor while you cut it up, and we'll find the hide and guts out back in the woods. Maybe all you did was possess venison beyond the ninety days after the closed season. How about it?"

It took George mere seconds to mull this over. "Yeah. Yeah! That's it. I kept those tenderloins too long. Write me up for that!"

The summons was issued and George thanked us as we left, saying that he'd meet us at the courthouse to settle up the next Friday.

Walking to the patrol car but still well within earshot Bart said in a loud voice, "Let's go thank Dizzy. He was a real help!"

George pled guilty to possession of whitetail deer during the closed season and paid slightly over fifteen hundred dollars in fines and costs. During lunch at the Big Boy restaurant Sergeant Bart smiled across the table and asked, "Do you feel better now?"

"Yes, much better," I replied. I'm just not used to "leaning" on people like you did with George. I don't think the locals would take it all that well."

"Right. George is used to that. That's the way they do it in Chicago," said Bart. "But Dizzy's name is going to be "Mud" with those Chicago boys figuring him to be our eye witness."

As the years passed, my mind has returned often to that warm foggy night, and I wonder how things might have turned out had I done things differently. Could I have successfully arrested the whole group of poachers? Probably so, but would it have been worth the potential violence I might have encountered? I guess not. Maybe there is a word somewhere between "Courage" and "Coward" called "Common sense".

_ςଠ_

Nubbins

Commercial fishing has always been an important industry for the states surrounding the Great Lakes. Minnesota, Wisconsin, Illinois, Indiana, Michigan, Ohio, Pennsylvania, New York and Canada all compete for their piece of the economic pie to be harvested from these fertile inland fresh water seas. Laws governing the species, sizes, and methods of taking fish can vary greatly from state to state and territorial borders are often jealously guarded by those who enforce these regulations.

Michigan and Wisconsin share a border in the waters of Green bay. Commencing at the middle of the Menominee River between the sister cities of Menominee, Michigan and Marinette, Wisconsin the State line extends out into Green Bay in a southeasterly direction to the approximate middle of the Bay. From there the line turns to the northeast to divide the Bay between the two states. Determining the location of this line is relatively easy during the winter months when one can take a compass reading and mark the border with old Christmas trees as is often done by Wisconsin's commercial gill netters.

One of the main differences in fishing regulations between Michigan and Wisconsin is that Wisconsin allows the use of gill nets in the taking of certain species such as Herring and White-fish, whereas Michigan does not. While very few Michigan commercial fishermen ply the border waters close to the state line, Wisconsin gill netters from Marinette tend to hug the state line in an effort to have an open side to the north, their net un-obstructed by neighboring competitive nets on the north side. At times a netter will set too close and actually cross the line. If detected by a Michigan Conservation Officer the net will be confiscated and the offender cited for fishing with an illegal device. Nets confiscated in this violation are usually condemned by the court and not returned to the fisherman.

Occasionally during the summer months a net will be set across the state line without the marking buoys required by Wisconsin law. These nets are set for the purposeful illegal taking of fish and are very hard to detect and enforce. Sometimes a fisherman just makes a mistake and sets his net too close, inadvertently encroaching into Michigan. It is up to the officer to determine whether or not the violation was intentional.

The early June morning mist was still on the water as Arnie piloted the commercial fish enforcement vessel, PB-4, out of the Menominee harbor and motored the short distance south to the state line. On the after deck I had just finished casting off and coiling the mooring lines. Life was good. You just can't beat a warm Green Bay morning on the deck of PB-4, cupping chilled fingers around a mug of hot chocolate, joking with Arnie, grinding our way along into a new adventure.

The state line was easily located with the new Loran-C locator. Prior to GPS, Loran navigation was state of the art. Radio towers spaced many miles apart were the basis of this system. A receiving device on the boat would pick up the signals sent from several of the towers and calculate the length of time it took to receive the signals, using triangulation to determine the location of the vessel. This system was accurate within several yards, and was accepted by the courts as admissible evidence.

Slowly patrolling our way out into Green Bay along the state line, Arnie kept a close eye on the fish finder for signs that would indicate a gill net crossing the line. Within half a mile Arnie shouted "Get the grapple out!" There on the graph we could see the telltale shadow of something looking suspiciously like a net crossing directly under the boat.

Circling back around for another pass we lowered the heavy grapple off the stern of the boat and began our "drag". The grapple is a device, usually made from heavy chain with hooks welded to a number of the links. When pulled along the bottom through the water the grapple serves to snag nets or other items sought to be retrieved. This drag proved to be a short trip, snagging a Whitefish net on the first pass. The net was untied and separated at the state line. The Wisconsin portion was anchored and marked with a buoy. The portion which extended into Michigan was fastened to the gill net lifter and we proceeded to seize the now illegal device.

A gill net resembles a large volleyball net with lead weights along the bottom rope and cork or plastic floats spaced along the top. Diamond shaped lacing of nylon or monofilament line forms the net between the floats and weights, serving to capture fish by their gills as they attempt to swim through the net. These nets can vary greatly in length, from as short as a hundred feet to as long as a mile or more. The net we were pulling this day was fairly wide and would have caught fish within eight feet of the lake bottom. The absence of fish in the net indicated that it had been set only recently, making its retrieval swift and easy. The mist, soon to burn off shortly after sunrise, reduced visibility to a few hundred feet as we pulled our way out into the Michigan fog.

It wasn't long before we could hear the faint rumble of an engine. As the sound of the motor grew louder it became obvious that the vessel we were hearing would be in the proximity of the net we were pulling. Soon we could make out the outline of an old, gray gill net tug bobbing in the mist. She seemed to be barely afloat, listing to portside and rocking heavily in the waves. The engine, an antique Ford flat head V-8 threatened to stall at any moment. From the hold of the boat we could hear what sounded like an argument of biblical proportions.

"For Christ's sake, keep the boat steady! Can't you do anything right?!"

"Aw shut your big mouth! If you don't like it, YOU come up here and drive this boat! Keep that net out of the prop! You snag a bucket with the twine and we'll be in a FINE mess!"

It was a man arguing with a woman. Mesmerized by the entertainment, Arnie and I stopped the net lifter and listened to the high level discussion which went on without stopping. The two dueling streams of salty language and criticism continued as the gill net slowly emanated out the stern of the tug, over the rollers and into the water. It soon became apparent that this couple was used to this type of dialogue, their life more or less one long, constant argument.

We would learn that the fisherman was known as "Nubbins", one of the oldest commercial fishermen on the Great Lakes. He and his wife had plied these waters most of their married lives, fighting and scrapping day after day as they pulled a living out of the lake. While seeming to be killing mad at each other, it was a sort of "singing inside" type of anger; just their way of life and one would have been lost without the other.

Arnie finally broke the spell with a blast from the air horn which captured the attention of Nubbins. We lifted the remaining net between his vessel and ours as Nubbins shut off his boat.

"Sir," said Arnie. "You have a little problem. Right now you're a quarter mile into Michigan."

"What?! Are you sure?" exclaimed Nubbins. "Well, what can you expect with Fatso driving the boat?"

Nubbins was joined at the stern door by his wife. While not exactly a 'fatso' Rosemary was built for work, her form reminiscent of 'Tugboat Annie', the television series from years ago. With broad, calloused hands ending in red, work hardened fingers, one could tell at a glance that she was no stranger to hard labor in adverse conditions.

"What did you get us into now?" shouted Rosemary.

"It's YOU, you big Bimbo!" shouted Nubbins in return. "You can't keep a straight course for love nor money! Might as well have a drunk at the helm!"

"Hey, hey," I interrupted. "Let us conduct our business and you two can settle this once Arnie and I are on our way."

Nubbins was cited for fishing with an illegal device and his net separated at the stern of his boat.

"Are you gonna keep that net?" asked Nubbins, pointing to the confiscated net aboard our boat.

"I'm going to have to give it some thought," I said. "I'll get back with you on that."

Nubbins paid his fine within a few days, requesting that I call him concerning the disposition of his net. The next day I pulled into Nubbin's yard. Ancient wooden fish boxes and several rotted row boats lay off to the side of the yard. A drying reel holding several hundred yards of antique cotton gill nets gave evidence of days gone down. Nubbins stepped from his net shed, squinting in the afternoon sun as he watched my approach. His expression brightened as he recognized the boxes of gill net in the bed of the pickup.

"Are ya really bringin' them back?" he asked incredulously.

"If you don't have them, I can't catch ya with 'em again," I laughed.

My short stop to drop off the net became several hours of visiting, talking of commercial fishing in years gone by, of fishing with cotton nets that now were ineffective and would not catch fish. Equipment and markets had changed many times over the years, and Nubbins had lived through them all. Seeing Nubbins and I sitting on the tailgate of the pickup, soaking up the warm early summer sun, Rosemary brought out coffee and cookies. A good time was had by everyone.

Years have passed and more changes have come to be. PB-4 has been retired from the lakes along with the officers who worked with her. Arnie has since passed away and gone to patrol the bountiful lakes in a better place. The iron men in their wooden boats have been replaced with modern equipment and businessmen. But I will always fondly remember the morning that Nubbins and Rosemary argued and scrapped their way across the Michigan/Wisconsin line.

Bring Them Home

ight rain speckled the patrol car's windshield, just a little too heavy for the intermittent wipers, not quite heavy enough for the full time 'slow' option. I was alternating between the two, wishing that some station on the radio would offer more lively music. VCO Nate was not very talkative on this dreary, cold late October Sunday afternoon. Occasionally glancing across in his direction I could see him gazing out the side window, trying to stay awake, as was I. The entire weekend had been too cold and rainy for off road vehicle recreation, and the only activity would have to be road hunting for grouse from vehicles. In the past three hours since lunch there had been no hunters encountered on the west county back roads to break our monotonous patrol. I was at the point of suggesting that we 'head for the barn' and call it a day, when Big Ben at the Stephenson State Police Post brought us back to the realm of the wakeful.

"Two-one-thirty-one from eight-nine, your location?"

"Shakey Lakes dam, eight-nine."

"Can you stop in at the Dan Gates residence and make sure that he's okay? His son just called saying that he hasn't heard from him in two days."

"Affirmative, eight-nine," I answered. "We're only a few miles from the location. Our ETA will be about ten minutes."

"Station eight-nine is clear," concluded Ben.

Dan Gates lived alone in a small home approximately a half mile off the highway just north of Shakey Lakes. Since the passing of his wife some ten years earlier he had resisted the efforts of his children to persuade him to move into the senior housing apartments in Stephenson. Having been a self-employed carpenter for most of his working life, he had very little in the way of retirement. He lived a simple life on his twenty remote, wooded acres; raising a large garden and do-ing small remodeling projects for his neighbors. I often suspected that he may have taken an occasional deer during the closed season, but for some unknown reason I just never got around to checking it out.

The well-worn sand road into Dan's home was muddy but passable as we slowly wound our way through the dripping forest. Sodden Red Oak leaves stuck to the windshield as a stiff breeze shook them from the trees, pushed to the side by the wipers and piling up on the sides of the glass.

"There's his house now," said Nate as we rounded the last curve and pulled into Dan's yard.

Dan was in front of his house, bent over as he placed a bag of fertilizer into his wheel barrow. As he had been doing for the past two days. I knew now why his son had asked the State Police to conduct a well-being check instead of coming up from Menominee and checking for themselves. During the rainy weekend, Dan should have been inside, where he would have answered the phone. His son had to have suspected that something was seriously amiss. He did not want to discover that his father had passed on, and found it easier to hear it from the authorities.

Dan's expression appeared calm, as if nothing were amiss. If not for the lack of pulse one might easily assume that he had merely decided to rest for a few seconds before continuing with his project. Dan's collie dog, cold and shivering, was soaked through with icy rain water. Though it could have gone through the open front door and into the house for shelter, it had not left its master's side for the entire time.

After calling Station eight-nine and advising them that Dan was no longer among the living, Nate and I carried Dan into the house, lay him on the couch and covered him with a quilt from the bedroom. As with many single elderly people, Dan had a bulletin board above his wall telephone showing numerous frequently called numbers. While Nate fed the dog I began calling friends and family, delivering the sad news of Dan's passing. Dan had lived a long, fruitful, happy life and had died peacefully. I couldn't see this as a tragedy.

One of the responsibilities assumed by police agencies is that of searching for lost or missing persons. Often the lost are found before a search can be organized. Unfortunately there are times when a person is late in returning home because they are no longer alive. The search then becomes a body recovery and it is rarely a happy occasion. If there is an upside to this it might be that, through the years, I have learned that dying is not always an unpleasant experience. When a person passes at the end of a normal, healthy life they usually show very little or no evidence of pain or suffering, especially if the death occurs at a location the person loved. Dan Gates appeared to be doing what he loved, tending his lawn and garden. In his case, death was merely something that got in the way of his lawn fertilizing project. His concern would have been more for his faithful dog than for himself. I was never comfortable with the term 'body recovery'. I chose to call it 'Bringing them home'.

I do believe that there are times when a person who may be nearing their life's end, realizes that their time is at hand and chooses the place to enjoy their last few moments. Such was the case of Mr. Cartwright.

The phone rang just before bed time on that cold January night. At least this time I was awake.

"Wayne," said sergeant Chipetti at the Stephenson Post. "Troopers Luis and Rob are down on county road 338, just a half mile west of M-35. Old Mr. Cartwright hasn't come back from rabbit hunting, and they need you to go in and find him."

"What's wrong with Louie and Rob going in?" I asked.

"They say you know the territory. They don't have snow boots, either," answered Sgt Chipetti.

The mercury was hovering at minus 12 degrees as I pulled up behind the blue patrol car and met Louie and Rob along highway 338. The area is surrounded by several sections of deep cedar swamp, usually too wet to walk. The frozen forest floor would have made for easy travel if it had not been for the knee deep snow.

"Hi Wayne," said Trooper Louie. "Mr. Cartwright parked his pickup and went into the swamp here on the north side. You can see the tracks of him and his dog."

A cursory look into the Cartwright truck revealed a cloth gun case and an open box of twenty gauge number seven shot shells. About half the box was missing. Tracks leading into an old logging road on the north side of the highway revealed those of a single person and a very small dog.

"The dog's tracks aren't those of one big enough to be hunting," I said. "I think we'll be carrying Mr. Cartwright back out. Something is not right here."

"Why didn't you bring your snow mobile?" asked Rob.

"I do not like snow mobiles, it's too thick in this swamp for anything but walking, and you're going to be walking with me," I answered.

"Oh no, we don't have boots," said Louie.

"Oh, but you do," I said as I took two pairs of zippered snow boots from the back seat of the patrol car.

Walking was difficult and progress slow as we negotiated the many blow down cedars across the trail and waded through the snow. At times the tracks revealed that the small dog had been walking through the snow. But most of the time the absence of tracks indicated that Mr. Cartwright was carrying the pet. Mr. Cartwright, a man in his eighties, seemed to be covering the ground quite rapidly, seldom stopping or turning from the path as hunters usually do.

We had covered nearly half a mile when my eye caught a reflection of some small shiny object a hundred yards ahead through the swamp.

"I think I see him," I told Rob and Louie who followed several paces behind. "Let's go slowly. I don't know what we'll find."

Mr. Cartwright sat on a low cedar stump, facing west with the shotgun across his lap. His small beagle pup leaned against his chest, wagging his tail apprehensively. The look on Mr. Cartwright's face was serene, his gaze at something far off in the distance, across an open cutoff clearing. This would have been the location of the sunset, several hours ago. A check of his pulse indicated that all life was gone from this proud old pioneer.

I left Louie and Rob to conduct their investigation and continued the remaining half mile north to Francour Lane. A resident neighbor answered my knock and offered the use of a plastic toboggan to transport Mr. Cartwright out to the road. Shortly the rescue squad, Rob, Louie, myself and Mr. Cartwright all met at the end of the trail where Mr. Cartwright was pronounced deceased and transported to the funeral home. To this day I remain convinced that Mr. Cartwright somehow sensed that his time was near and decided to spend his last afternoon watching one last sunset in his favorite hunting swamp with his little Beagle friend. It was my honor to bring this gentleman home.

Another cold December evening found VCO Pete and me returning to the State Police Post just in time to answer a well-being check at the Bergland farm a mile east of the post. Stanley Bergland had been cutting dead elm for firewood in a creek bottom forty acres or so north of the house and had not returned for supper. Anticipating travel over rough ground, Pete and I borrowed the forestry division four wheel drive pickup and sallied forth to the Bergland residence.

Mrs. Bergland was beside herself with worry. "I just know something bad has happened." she cried. "If it's a heart attack, I can accept that. He's in his seventies and his heart is not what used to be. But I couldn't stand it if he's pinned under some tree, suffering!"

"Now don't you worry ma'am," I said. "Whatever it is, Pete and I will handle it. I can't promise you good news, but we'll do our best."

The trip to the firewood area was easy, with a well-worn two track road across the field to the edge of the swamp. Several large dead elm trees lay abut, all felled in an easterly direction, indicating that they had more than likely all been dropped during the same period of time, with the wind from the west. Near the center of the small valley, along the bank of the dry creek, lay Stan Bergland. It was evident that he had sensed something coming on; perhaps a heart attack, maybe a stroke. He had lay down on the ground rather than fallen, and assumed the position of one taking a short nap, as innocent as a child. His expression was that of a man totally at rest. He had lived his life, cut his last firewood, and it was time to go; so he did.

Pete and I placed him in the bed of the pickup and covered him with a bright yellow highway emergency blanket. The ride back to the Bergland home was a cold one, with Pete driving and me riding guard in the pickup box with Stan. The medical examiner had been summoned and had already made Mrs. Bergland aware of the passing of her husband. I would describe the situation to her soon.

Crossing the cold, dark windswept field my mind conjured up the crazy image of Stan arriving in heaven, meeting long lost hunting friends and saying "Put the coffee on, Boys. The day is done, the firewood is cut, and I'm headed home in a DNR pickup alongside the game warden!" Or was it such a crazy thought? When my time comes, I hope that God is as kind to me.

Stan's widow agreed.

The Good Neighbor

The knock was nearly imperceptible, and I was not sure that I had even heard it. Turning from the paperwork at my cluttered desk I looked out the front window of our living room. There in the bright spring morning sunshine stood an old, green, rusty Chevrolet three quarter ton pickup, complimenting the potholes and mud of my neglected clay and sand driveway.

Visits to the Game Warden's residence, at least in the Upper Peninsula are common. Usually they are heralded by the noisy splash of an impatient driver trying to empty my mud puddles in one swat, and the insistent banging of a fist on our poor, beleaguered front door. The attitude of "Hey, hurry up and serve me!" was not unusual. This form of impatience was often displayed by members of the public, wanting full bang for their license or tax dollar. No problem, it goes with the territory. Come on in and tell me your problem, and we'll see how this all shakes out. But getting into my driveway without being heard, now *that* took some patience and finesse. The nearly silent knock at the door set me to wondering what new adventure lurked behind the threshold.

The opening of the front door revealed a very large, humble looking man. By today's standards where we see six foot-six, four hundred pound specimens of manhood frolicking around the grandstands at truck pulls this fellow would not have stood out. But back in the late nineteen seventies when everyone stood in awe of the largess of Hoss Cartwright, this man was a giant. With his head slightly bowed and hands folded before him he appeared to be almost apologetic for intruding upon my day.

"Uh, sorry, sorry to bodder you," he stammered. "I uh, just wanted to uh, stop and say 'Hi'. You stopped me and my brudder last deer season, and you treated us very well."

"Come on in and sit down. I'm sure you know me as Wayne Coleman," I said, stepping back and offering a chair.

"Oh tank you, tank you, no. I just wanted to say tanks for being so nice. I'm Frankie. My Fadder named me a girl's name, so my friends just call me Frankie."

I was having trouble with remembering an incident wherein this fellow was involved. A short conversation brought out that it was one of those momentary encounters during the deer season when I was standing by the roadside, preparing to re-enter the patrol car after checking a hunter in a deer blind at the wooded edge of a farm field. Frankie must have taken my friendly wave as a signal to stop. Small talk about the hunting conditions had been understood by Frankie as a "check", and Frankie was impressed that I hadn't searched his car or asked to look in his trunk. Years later it would come out that he had an untagged doe in the trunk and was attempting to sneak it home. No big deal. It wasn't the first time I'd been snookered.

Frankie presented me with a pint of honey from a beekeeping friend, which I accepted with gratitude. Many kind words and several handshakes later Frankie departed, leaving me wondering why anyone would go so far out of their way to show appreciation for just doing my job.

"Just be happy that someone appreciates what you do," said Katheryne. "You put too much thought into everyday things. He's probably been treated poorly in the past, and appreciates your fairness. He's probably lonesome, living alone like he does. Maybe he just needs a friend."

During the ensuing months Frankie and I did indeed become friends. His shyness had undoubtedly been caused by his great size and his backwoods way of speaking. I'm sure that grade school kids had teased him about being a "Fatty, fatty two-by-four" and probably bullied him physically. His father had been domineering and cruel, often beating Frankie and his mother at the least provocation. Because of this, Frankie was very sensitive to what was said to him, often misinterpreting a friendly joke as an insult. Being his friend was going to be a challenge.

Frankie was one of the last of the single "Jobbers"; the men who would single handedly contract a timber cutting operation and conduct the project from start to finish. His glory days had been before the tree harvester, the shear, the skidder, and the cutting head. Corporate timber harvesting was still in the future, and a single man could pick up a chainsaw and make a decent living in the woods. In today's world a sawyer may still do piece cutting, but it is for a large harvesting operation and he is an employee rather than the owner of the company. In the years of our friendship I would see Frankie forced out of business for economic as well as health reasons.

Frankie was an enigma to say the least. At times I felt that I could better understand him with the help of an interpreter. Along with his manner of speaking, which tended to round off his words to "Dis, dat, dese, dem, and dose", many of his words were ambiguous attempts that required some thought to interpret, such as "idapopenin' for ibuprofen, or 'ert' for earth. Sometimes he spoke in riddles that only he understood.

One day he was describing the effects of a dynamite blast. "Yeah, what they say is true about dynamite taking all the oxygen away when it goes off. I blew out that wildlife pond and it killed the cat."

Frankie did not have an actual cat. I finally figured out that when he detonated the dynamite, he used the ignition of his small John Deere bulldozer which he referred to as his 'cat'. He must have used the coil wire instead of the starter post to touch off the blasting cap and stalled the engine. Frankie blamed the shutting off of the tractor on the dynamite explosion, some two hundred yards away. I couldn't convince him otherwise, so I just agreed with him.

Frankie loved children, and young Shawn and Becky were his favorites. With each visit he would bring treats for them on the order of candy bars and popsicles. As tactfully as possible I tried to impress upon Frankie the importance of a healthy diet, especially for youngsters. He finally acquiesced and began bringing apples and other fruits.

Frankie was delighted when Shawn reached the age of twelve, and could bow hunt. A special deer blind was set up in Frankie's yard and bait was set out every evening. Before season Shawn would get a telephoned report from Frankie each night detailing how big and how many visitors were at the bait. Frankie made sure that Shawn always had a snack before going out to the blind, and when Shawn arrowed his first deer, Frankie was beside himself with happiness.

Two years later Shawn hunted from Frankie's blind in the swamp. The first morning he shot a spike horn buck, and Frankie was literally jumping up and down with glee.

"Shawn's first deer! Shawn's first deer!" shouted Frankie as I arrived at his home.

"Aw, c'mon Frankie," said Shawn. "I've already taken two deer with a bow."

"Yeah, but *this* is with a *gun!*" shouted Frankie, still hopping about.

Frankie would never wear hunter orange while hunting deer as required by law. Despite my many attempts to convince him that deer do not see colors the same way as humans, he was undeterred. "You can see that there orange color a mile away. You can't tell me the deer don't see that," he would argue. One day during the second week of deer season I made him an offer.

"Okay Frankie," I said. "Here's what I'll do. Tomorrow I'll sit out in the middle of your front yard dressed from head to foot in hunter orange. Cap, coat, pants and gloves. I'll shoot a deer in plain sight, and it won't run from the color. If that happens, you'll have to wear orange when hunting deer from now on."

"Alright," said Frankie with a smile. "We'll just see what happens."

The next afternoon I was in position on a folding chair, smack in the middle of Frankie's driveway. The long entrance drive to his home extended up the wooded hill for nearly a quarter mile where it intersected a ninety degree turn in the gravel county road. The yard was surrounded by pine and aspen forest, with Frankie's house approximately one hundred yards north of my folding chair seat.

As the afternoon sun began to dip below the western tree line a spike horn buck stepped out onto the driveway to the south at a distance of about seventy yards. I dropped it where it stood with one shot from my grandfather's old 35 Remington. There went my buck tag.

"No fair," said Frankie as I dressed out the deer. The deer was too far away. It couldn't see you."

"A deal is a deal Frank," I said. I told you I'd get a deer wearing orange, and I did it. You're going to have to start wearing orange from now on."

"No, no, it wasn't fair," complained Frankie.

"Okay, let's do this again tomorrow and see what happens," I suggested.

"Sure, we'll see them run tomorrow," said Frankie.

The next evening was like the first, with a cold nip in the air and very little breeze. I had been sitting on the folding chair for a half an hour when the brush cracked immediately behind me. Turning in the chair and bending my neck as far to the right as possible I beheld a large doe standing on the lawn a mere twenty yards behind my position. The old chair creaked as I slowly swiveled around and took aim. The doe dropped at the thundering crack of the old thirty-five and my antlerless tag was spent. Frankie came from the house to witness the tagging of this beautiful animal.

"Now what do you say, Frankie?" I asked. "That deer could not have helped but see me this time."

"Well, there was something wrong with that deer," retorted Frankie. "No normal deer would stand there and just let you shoot it with all that orange there."

A guy just couldn't win. It was finally my son who convinced Frankie to put on an orange cap to hunt. Shawn simply refused to hunt with anyone who did not follow the law.

On another afternoon I had decided to accept Frankie's invitation to bow hunt in a blind set at the southeast corner of his yard. Upon arrival I was greeted by an apologetic Frankie who said, "I'm really sorry, I put a different colored canvass on the wood pile this afternoon. We won't see any deer for a couple of weeks. Any new thing throws them off."

"I wouldn't worry about that, Frankie," I replied. "Just a few days ago we watched from your living room as two does walked right up to my car and sniffed at it. That was something new."

"Well, deer don't pay attention to cars," replied Frankie. (Arrrrrrgh!)

Frankie was plagued with numerous health problems, mostly because of his weight. Incessant snacking kept him at something well over three hundred pounds. I often wished that I could take Frankie along with me on patrol, or some recreational trip, but his weight simply prevented it. Any suggestion that he might feel better, live longer and just be healthier was mis-interpreted as teasing and he often took offense at any concern I might show relating to his obesity. One afternoon I briefly felt that he might finally be on the right track. It was one of those blustery February days when outdoor patrol would have been unproductive; a fool's journey in fact. Frankie had come over to my shop to have me change the oil in his pickup. As I fiddled about under the engine, dodging drips of dirty salt water and cursing Andy Williams who vocally expounded on the radio about this being the "most wonderful time of the year", Frankie sat on a sturdy iron chair conversing about the usual everyday life things that friends talk about; just life in general.

"I had just toast for breakfast this morning," said Frankie, the surprise of which caused me to momentarily forget my location and attempt to sit up, smacking my forehead on the rusty sway bar.

"Really Frank!" I exclaimed, rubbing my bruised forehead and trying to pre-delete a few expletives. "That's great!"

"Yep. Twenty-one pieces. Lotsa Butter and jam," said Frankie, proud as punch.

For years I had been trying to convince Frankie to have his right hip replaced. It was getting so that our every visit con-sisted of a detailed rundown of all his aches and pains. At my suggestion that he look into hip surgery, Frankie always balked.

"I don't want them to go in and just start hacking away!" Frankie would complain.

"Listen Frankie," I would say. "I've had three back surger-ies. None of them have been fun. But If I hadn't gone under the knife I wouldn't be walking today. Those surgeons don't get paid thousands of dollars to mess up. They know what they're doing. Now I can work. I can fight if I have to. I can run. What can you do with that bad hip?"

"Well, I want to wait until I absolutely have to before I go in," He would say. My reply was always the same.

"If you had a rod knocking in your car, what would you do?"

"I'd have it fixed," He would say.

"Then go get fixed!" I would admonish. There was no convincing him. We would have to just wait until the bad situation got worse.

The time finally came when Frankie could not stand the pain any more. One afternoon as I tinkered on Frankie's truck I listened with half an ear as he nattered on about his health problems. Suddenly I heard him talking about suicide.

"...And that big oak tree west of my place at the curve? That's going to be my target. If I hit that thing dead center I won't last long. The pain will be all over with. I want you to have my meat grinder and my..."

My heart was in my throat. Loudly slamming the hood of his truck I interrupted him with a blast that would have shocked a wounded Rhino.

"Listen here, you big baboon!" I shouted. "If you kill yourself I'll throw your big, fat butt in jail! It's illegal to commit suicide. Don't you *ever* talk about breaking the law around me!" I was at the end of my rope. All the concerned pleas had done no good. To my surprise Frankie threw up his hands and rocked back on his chair, nearly falling back onto the greasy cement floor.

"I'm sorry! I'm sorry!" pleaded Frankie, tears streaming down his reddened cheeks. "I won't do it! I'll go see the doctor!"

Why didn't I try that before?

Appointments were made, doctor visits became frequent, and the day for surgery was set three months in the future. Frankie was going to be able to donate his own blood, one pint per month, to be used if necessary during surgery.

The day of his first blood donation was a small gala affair. I stopped by his house to wish him well on his trip to the Marquette blood bank, from which he would return that night.

Several other neighbors and friends had also dropped by to see him off on the start of his adventure. Upon his return I again visited him to see how things went.

"Oh they had to stop," said Frankie. "I began shaking like a leaf, I got the chills, I was sweating bullets, my blood pressure shot sky high and I got pale as a ghost."

No stranger to blood and platelet donation, I found it difficult to believe that such a strapping big fellow would have trouble donating blood. "Wow, that's quite a reaction," I said. "How much blood did they get before they had to stop?"

"Oh, they didn't even get the needle in," he said.

The surgery went forth, but Frankie had let the hip damage progress too far for the operation to be a success. After his recovery Frankie managed to get from the wheel chair to the bathroom, and to get around the kitchen enough to prepare a few meals, but the die was cast. Within several months he was committed to a nursing home where he lived his last few years confined to his bed.

When I was promoted and assigned to the downstate harbor town of Rogers City, Frankie took it very personally. He could not hide the fact that his feelings were deeply hurt, actually accusing me of suddenly deciding to 'not like' him. Every visit was a guilt trip, where I would be subjected to a rant of how I was inconsiderately abandoning him, and that his life may just as well be over with my running off without a thought for his feelings. Moving to my new assignment was almost a relief. Still I could not help missing the good years of his friendship and generosity.

The next fall I received word that Frankie was failing and that his time was short. The journey back to Menominee County was a long one, with many memories coming to mind. Just west of Escanaba I pulled into the hospital and looked up his room number on the register.

Frankie was resting comfortably and looked better than I had anticipated. He talked slowly, with a weak voice; probably from the pain killers. We spoke at some length about the 'good old days', of deer hunting, and our times together while I repaired his machinery. As the afternoon wore on we relived many experiences, talked about our friends, talked about everything except the fact that soon Frankie would no longer be among the living and my hunting partner of many years would be gone. The sun began casting long shadows through his window and we both knew that we'd soon be running out of things to say. Suddenly he extended his hand to be shaken and said in a strong voice, "Goodbye, old friend!"

With tears welling up in my eyes I fell forward, giving him a hug that two old woodsmen might share, each knowing that they will never see each other again. It tore at my heart, but I knew it was time to go. Turning so that Frankie would not see the tears, I left his room. I left the hospital knowing that Frankie and I had had a good run as friends go, and that I'll go a long way before I find another good neighbor like him.

Old Man River

The late October afternoon sun dipped low over the Wisconsin horizon as I stood on the Chalk Hills Bridge on Snow Road. Behind me the mighty Chalk Hills dam roared, all generators on line, two of the overflow gates wide open, wasting water from the heavy rainfall of the previous week. Beneath me the Menominee River flowed deep and swift. An occasional log, loosened by high water, drifted past on its slow journey to its eventual destination in Green Bay some forty miles downstream. Brown oak leaves blew into the stream from shore and danced on the silver surface of the water.

I have always thought of the Menominee river as miniature Mississippi, always flowing, always patient, always there; sometimes peaceful, sometimes raging; sometimes reassuring and restful, other times frightening and dangerous. Much of my career has been spent on this waterway and its depths hold hundreds of memories.

A hundred yards to my left the intersection of Chalk Hills road and Snow Road marks the place where VCO Nate and I encountered a dirt bike and four ORV's one summer Sunday afternoon, coming down the middle of the gravel road, not a helmet in the group. The dirt bike spun out in an effort to escape and the four wheelers fled down the road to the south. After citing the biker for no helmet and issuing a warning for operating an unlicensed vehicle on the highway, VCO Nate and I drove slowly to the south to where tracks from the 4 wheelers turned into the forest. Following the ORV tracks we ran them down on foot where the logs and debris on the forest floor became too rough to operate the vehicles.

Another quarter mile to the south I once cited a fisherman in possession of three undersized Walleye. The dead fish were kept in an otherwise empty plastic pail, barely large enough to fillet; seriously undersized. As I wrote the citation, the guilty party, in an effort to destroy the evidence, grabbed the fish and sprinted toward the river. The fish were saved for evidence but not before we wrestled on the ground in a campsite fire pit, both of us becoming blackened with soot and ashes. The prosecutor later dismissed the ticket without conferring with me when the fisherman complained of excessive force. Upon my suggestion, the prosecutor read the police report and apologized for not having called me, saying that he would have never dismissed the case had he known all the facts. Not unusual, it happened frequently with some prosecutors, but that's another story.

Looking downstream I could see the northernmost tip of Merriman Island, the only Michigan Island in the river, south of Pemine falls. Back in the early 1980's Wisconsin deer hunters had been boating across, hunting the island without the required Michigan nonresident deer licenses. One cold, sunny late November afternoon Fire Division Supervisor Joe Noah and I canoed from the Rosebush access site over to the island, breaking the new ice as we went. Once on the island the challenge was to hike the forty odd acres of oak forest and locate the illegal hunters. Joe stayed with the canoe to ward off any potential escapees.

A total of four Wisconsin residents were apprehended in the three hours before darkness. All were cited for hunting deer without a license. On my return across the island I noticed that the temperature had dropped considerably and my ears, nose and fingers were beginning to complain of threatening frostbite. Following a bright orange glow in the vicinity of the canoe I discovered that Joe had built a most welcome roaring campfire on the shore. The granola bars in Joe's pockets made a fine snack as I warmed my tingling extremities. The voyage through the night back to the mainland was uneventful although somewhat tedious, having to break new ice.

The next fall found me back at the island with my son, Shawn. A complainant had called before sunrise saying that two unlicensed duck hunters had made plans to hunt the eastern shore of Merriman Island. There was no time to call a VCO, so I gave Shawn a quick shake and told him to put on some waterproof clothes.

The mid-October sun was just breaking in the east as Shawn and I rounded the middle point on the island's eastern shore. The small cove ahead to our left was occupied by two hunters in a short aluminum boat and a small raft of Mallard decoys.

"Let's get 'em!" I shouted to Shawn, and as we lay into the racing paddles the Hoefgen canoe shot forward. The two duck hunters began a panicked flurry of action, pulling the anchors and trying to start the motor. Leaving their decoys behind, they actually got the five horse motor running and the boat underway as Shawn and I glided up to them and halted their retreat. I wished that my son and I could have worked together more.

Gazing to the southeast along the shore I could almost hear the loud music and drunken shouts of the revelers at the many drinking parties that took place during the summer of 1985. Random campfires, littering and the cutting of live trees had become so prevalent that Wisconsin Power company authorities found it necessary to post some of their shoreline property against recreational use, and requested that the trespass law be enforced. Many nights were spent on foot patrol with VCO's Nate, Wade and Pete, intercepting drinking parties of underage teens. Numerous citations were issued throughout the summer for trespass and littering until the rate of compliance reached an acceptable level.

Just out of sight to the south stood the White Rapids dam, one of the best Walleye fishing sites on the river. It was from this dam that our small 4-H challenge group embarked one spring afternoon for a short downstream canoe trip. Our float cruise in the sun was soon interrupted by a near fatal misfortune. An ice jam across the river at the Sturgeon Hole caught our group by surprise and very nearly capsized two of the canoes. Except for the skill of the canoeists, they could have been pulled beneath the jam and drowned. The line between safety and tragedy is sometimes very thinly drawn.

The sun was now below the horizon and darkness began to encroach upon my reverie. In the forest on the Wisconsin side of the river a Barred owl asked "Who cooks for you? Who cooks for y-o-o-o-u-u-u?" It was time to move along. But I remained yet a few moments more, lost in thought. Just a few miles of river, and yet all those memories, and many more. It's easy to see how life is often compared to a river, rolling on over the dam, under the bridge, much of it going on unnoticed until one stops to remember. The river flows on, the memories fade into the past and we refer to them as "the good old days". Some day today will be "the good old days". Let's enjoy them while we can.

About the Author

Wayne Coleman was born and spent his childhood in the county of Alpena, Michigan. His love of the out of doors and the inspiration of two Conservation Officers early in life led him to pursue the life of a Michigan Game Warden. His dream became a reality in 1977 upon being assigned as a Conservation Officer in Menominee County in Michigan's Upper Peninsula. The path to the realization of his dream included service in the United States Army, a tour in Vietnam, and six years as a State park Ranger. Wayne enjoys the retired life in Newaygo, Michigan with his patient wife, two cats and a dog.

Made in the USA
San Bernardino, CA
27 June 2015